Prone to Wander
A Woman's Struggle with Sexual Sin and Addiction

Co-Authors
Sabrina D. Black, MA, LLPC, CAC-I
LaVern A. Harlin, BA

Prone to Wander Series

*Priority*ONE
p u b l i c a t i o n s
Detroit, MI USA

Published in association with:
PriorityONE Publications, P. O. Box 725, Farmington, Michigan 48332-0725

ISBN 0-9703634-1-9

Cover Design by: Chris Ortiz Reignlife@aol.com
Typesetting by: Sabrina D. Black, Christina Dixon
Edited by: Mary D. Edwards, Rev. Debra A. Nixon, PhD, Gina Behrens, Pat Hicks

Printed in the United States of America
Printed on Recycled Paper
Published October, 2003

Endorsements

*This fine volume, **"Prone to Wander,"** tackles an epidemic problem that plagues our society and the church. Black and Harlin address the matter Biblically and sensitively yet forthrightly and effectively. The depth of their exploration shows experience, expertise and careful documentation. With each burst of uncleanness comes a refreshing use of Scripture. Hope shines strong throughout the pages. And practical guidance can be gleaned from the sage advice.*

Bruce W. Fong, Ph.D.
President, Michigan Theological Seminary

✠   ✠   ✠   ✠   ✠   ✠   ✠   ✠   ✠   ✠

And God said, "Separate Sabrina & LaVern for the work I've called them to do." **Prone to Wander** *is an example of what happens when one ministers the gifts he or she has to others through the manifold grace of God [I Peter 4:10]. For every trial there is a matching grace. Pastors, prisoners, pilgrims & problem solvers will benefit from this classic resource.*

Rev. Haman Cross, Jr.
Pastor, Rosedale Park Baptist Church
Author, "Wild Thing," and "Maximum Sex Video Series"

✠   ✠   ✠   ✠   ✠   ✠   ✠   ✠   ✠   ✠   ✠   ✠

"Prone To Wander" is a hard tale to tell, but Black and Harlin rise above the shame and fear of self-disclosure and present themselves as living sacrifices. This book is a confrontation of love and readers will know that they are loved above everything. My response is to call my sister, my therapist, and my God.

Rev. Dr. Debra A. Nixon
Pastor, Liberation Church Ministries
Author, "Womanhood: A Journey Towards Love"

✠   ✠   ✠   ✠   ✠   ✠   ✠   ✠   ✠   ✠   ✠

"Prone to Wander" will heighten your sensitivity for administering God's grace more effectively to those who are struggling with sexual sin. Sabrina and LaVern, my sisters and fellow members of AACC have provided the body of Christ with a much-needed resource that provides a holistic approach to the issue of addictions.

Dr. Atty. Paris Finner-Williams
Author, "Marital Secrets: Dating, Communication Lies, and Sex"

✠   ✠   ✠   ✠   ✠   ✠   ✠   ✠   ✠   ✠   ✠   ✠

"Prone to Wander" is a uniquely compassionate and caring perspective on the plights of those who are addicted to sexual activity. This excellent compilation of theoretical and practical information is an invaluable resource to all students and practitioners in the field of mental health and pastoral counseling.

Bishop Ned Adams, Jr., Ph.D.
Senior Pastor, True Faith Church International

Prone to Wander:
A Woman's Struggle with Sexual Sin and Addiction

TABLE OF CONTENTS

Prone to Wander:
A Woman's Struggle with Sexual Sin and Addiction
Sabrina D. Black, MA, LLPC, CAC-I
LaVern A. Harlin, BA

Preface

Prone to Wander, Lord, we feel it and so do many others. Not only have many felt the lure of sexual sins, but also many have gone astray and need to be restored. We praise God for breaking the bondage in our lives and in the lives of our clients. We understand the importance of sharing our stories as part of shattering the outer man so that the Spirit of God (the inner man) may be fully released. The failures and the victories have been critical in helping us to understand our journey and the plight of those who have had similar struggles with sexual sin.

Whenever we would talk about breaking the silence by putting our stories in print, our hearts would pound rapidly as we heaved for air, trying not to hyperventilate. Guilt and shame have kept us and many others shackled, and in bondage.

When we first began this project, we were hard pressed to remember what it was like to live a totally entangled lifestyle. We were caught in a web of lies and deception, totally consumed by the desire for more and more. There was a void in life that we sought to fill through means that now seem unimaginable. We made choices and took risks that no one in his or her right mind would do. We were obviously not in our right minds, "the mind of Christ Jesus." During the time of our intense sexual struggle, which eventually led to addiction, each of us lived the secret sexual fantasies of many women and men.

Even after being physically delivered, there was a healing of the mind that needed to take place. Those thoughts constantly raced through our minds. Almost every sight, sound, touch, smell or person encountered would instantly trigger a memory or create a fantasy. But thanks be to God, He renewed our minds. Through His power, we have been able to cast down vain imaginations and take every thought captive.

This project has forced us to once again face the demons from which we have been delivered. The Lord has strengthened us to stand in the face of evil and to help set other captives free. As Christian mental health counselors, we have been able to work with people in bondage through individual, marital and group counseling. This book gives us an additional opportunity to break the silence and be a voice for women who struggle with sexual sin. We expose what has been done in darkness so that many others may see the light of Jesus Christ and be loosed from their shackles.

Sabrina D. Black, MA, LLPC, CAC-I
LaVern A. Harlin, BA
Co-Authors

Foreword

Heroism is rarely seen these days by Christians concerning their faith. Sabrina and LaVern have put together a courageous book on female struggles with sexuality and addiction. *Prone to Wander* cracks the door so that light can shine in on one of the farmost hidden closets in the church, female sexuality.

I believe that as this book reaches out to the hurting hearts that it was penned to touch, new life will spring out of the heart of the reader. *Prone to Wander* is clearly personal and professional. The compassion of the authors is felt throughout their work. As a fellow journeyer of recovery, I get a sense that Sabrina and LaVern have been down the same road that their readers have experienced.

It is often true that the Lord will take the dark corners of our life and make us stronger through them, so that He receives the glory. In our weakness He will become our strength. This is a reality for those of us who are wounded healers.

It is a privilege to have Sabrina and LaVern on God's team, to heal the sexually broken. I would encourage pastors, women's leaders, and those who have a heart for nurturing women to take the time to read *Prone to Wander*. This book can bring new life and healing to you or someone you know.

God is returning America back to sexual health. I am so encouraged that *Prone to Wander* addresses those who are sometimes forgotten, the women who feel damaged sexually.

I want to say, thanks again Sabrina and LaVern for creating a resource so that others can begin to heal.

God bless,

Doug Weiss, Ph.D.

Author of *The Final Freedom* and *She Has a Secret*

Acknowledgements

Thank you from us!

- To God for the abundance of grace He has extended toward us in the writing of this project. The Holy Spirit has guided us and made this work a finished product. To God be the glory!
- To our Family and Friends who supported us and encouraged us through many months of hard work. We want to express our appreciation to our parents: Clyde and Adell B. Dickinson, and Helen J. Harlin. They have nurtured us to make an impact in the world and a real difference to those we minister to.
- To Our clients; those who have been set free and those in the process of recovery – we are honored to walk along side you.
- To Latitia Watkins and Hivenna Crockett, our girlfriends who pray for us in the fulfillment of our calling and for understanding our passion.
- To Tony Ross and the "Girlfriends Who Know" Crew, The Rosedale Park Baptist Church Counseling Ministry Team, and The WRAP (Writers Resources for Accountability and Publishing) Group.
- To the Initial Preview Team: Roger and Dr. Lyn Johnson, Debby Mitchell, Linda Emptage, Laverne Phelps, Dr. Bruce Fong, Ron Horton, and Ramona Tillman (Sabrina's assistant)
- To the Final Preview Team: Makeisha Page, Patty Switaj, Letha Walls, Kim L. Patterson.
- To the Editors: Mary B. Edwards, Debra A. Nixon, PhD.
- To our Pastor Haman Cross, Jr. who has and always will be a mentor and visionary in our lives.
- To Matthew Parker—Lift Every Voice/Moody Imprint, and Jim Ruark-Zondervan, for encouraging us to finish the good work we had begun despite rejection.

Thank you from Sabrina

- To my husband, W. Jose' Black for all his encouragement, love and support. As well as creating a space for me to write.
- To Victoria Johnson for insisting that I tell the, "sex story" so that others can be set free.

Thank you from LaVern

- To the mighty men, my brothers (Kenneth, Terry, Edwin, Roy), for being a source of encouragement & a covering for me.

Book Overview

The overall goal of this book is to provide hope, help, and healing for women who are *"prone to wander"* and for those who minister to them. Many have felt the lure of sexual sins; many have gone astray and needed to be restored. This book provides Biblical and personal strategies for setting the captives free. A uniquely practical perspective, while caring and compassionate, on the plight of those who are struggling and trapped in sexual sin. ***Prone to Wander: A Woman's Struggle with Sexual Sin and Addiction*** is an invaluable resource for any woman who desires to be set free from the struggles, as well as for those who wish to understand her pain and assist her in the process. This book will bless women who are struggling with sexual sin, as well as clergy and counselors.

Introduction

"Prone to Wander, Lord, I feel it. Prone to leave the God I love. Here's my heart. O take and seal it. Seal it for thy courts above. "

Prone to Wander, is an innate feeling and experience that believers tend to have as they walk with God. Just like sheep, many have gone astray. The words to the old hymn, "Come thy Fount," provide some answers to the wandering of God's people. "Here's my heart. O take and seal it. Seal it for thy courts above." When we give our hearts over to God, He will seal them as we walk in victory not allowing our appetite to continue to wander away from God. Just as the Psalmist tells us in chapter 34 verse 8, we can "taste and see that the LORD is good: blessed is the man that trusteth in him." "He hath filled the hungry with good things." (Luke 1:53a)

This book will open windows of hope, help, and healing as you hear many stories of struggle, addiction, deliverance and redemption. The stories shared are ours, others', and even yours. We are excited about what God is doing and will do for you to break the bondage and silence of sexual sin and addiction.

Struggling with Sexual Sin

As we arrived at the counseling center one morning, the first order of business was a brief case consultation about a few clients before the busy day began. We opened with prayer and devotion through reading the Word of God. The focus was on life through the Spirit.

Therefore, there is now no condemnation for those who are in Christ Jesus because through Christ Jesus the law of the Spirit of life has set me free from the law of sin and death. For what the law was powerless to do in that it was weakened by the sinful nature, God did by sending his own Son in the likeness of sinful man to be a sin offering. And so he condemned sin in sinful man, in order that the righteous requirements of the law might be fully met in us, who do not live according to the sinful nature but according to the Spirit. Those who live according to the sinful nature have their minds set on what that nature desires; but those who live in accordance with the Spirit have their minds set on what the spirit desires. The mind of sinful man is death, but the mind controlled by the Spirit is life and peace: the sinful mind is hostile to God. It does not submit to God's law nor can it do so. Those controlled by the sinful nature cannot please God (Romans 8:1-8).

Before the last scripture was read both of us wept as we were reminded of God's saving grace and the power that set us free from sexual sin and the understanding of God's Word to walk in victory. We know from experience that God has set the captives free and we can be free indeed. Our desire is to do more than speak a message of hope, help and healing, but to live a lifestyle that incorporates that message. We are firsthand witnesses of what God can do.

I often heard the concept quoted, "Just say no." There were many days I said no, but my body said yes. Yes to pornography and to other sexual sin. I remember being in a vicious cycle of entrapment (not being able to let go and let God). I was reminded of Paul's struggle with sin. When he wanted to do right, he could not. This was the cycle in which I was caught.

So many of God's children are caught up in sexual sin and other addictions. By the Bible's standard, it is already declared an epidemic.

> *Do you not know that the wicked will not inherit the kingdom of God? Do not be deceived: Neither the sexually immoral nor idolaters nor adulterers nor male prostitutes nor homosexual offenders nor thieves nor the greedy nor drunkards nor slanderers nor swindlers will inherit the kingdom of God. And that is what some of you were. (I Corinthians 6:9-11)*

But you were washed, you were sanctified, the Spirit of our God justified you in the name of the Lord Jesus Christ.

In addition to giving you the courage to break the silence, this book will give you the confidence and commitment to choose freedom. He who the Son sets free is free indeed. We looked at the clock and realized our first clients were soon to arrive.

Kathy was prone to wander due to her appetite for love, attention, success and various hidden desires. She struggled, hoping her feelings were not true. She was in counseling because she wanted desperately to stop acting out sexually. Her behaviors were contrary to her traditional religious upbringing and violated many of the principles on which she once so faithfully lived.

3

She had an appetite that always said, "Feed me." The night before she had had sex with two different men within hours of each other. All the time she was thinking, "Where do I go next?" One of her sex partners was Jim, a casual acquaintance from work. Although they had become closer as a result of a recent project, she was not physically attracted to him in any way. This was the third night in a row that they had to work overtime. Kathy was really tired and wanted to be home with her husband and children. When Jim discovered a major error in the data on their reports, Kathy just burst into tears.

It was an awkward moment for both Jim and Kathy. As he reached out for her to provide some consolation, she collapsed into his arms in heavy sobs. He squeezed her tighter. When Kathy opened her eyes she realized that his body was pressing her body against the door to the office. She knew what was about to happen, but rationalized that she needed to do something—anything to reduce the stress and strain of the project. So with no regard for those waiting at home she gave in to the moment. For her it was really no big deal. This wasn't the first time she'd had sex with a co-worker to relieve the tension. That same evening she went home and had sex with her husband as if nothing had happened. Although her body went through the motion, she was not really present.

This appetite developed in her childhood and as an adult it was out of control. Kathy explained it was like being thirsty on a hot summer's day and never being able to quench her thirst. Sex and various sexual activities had become her answer for coping with pain or for seeking pleasure. Masturbation and pornography were like eating candy. Now her appetite had grown to weekly sexual encounters with co-workers and casual acquaintances. She had a simple message as she looked into our eyes; **HELP ME.**

Have you ever had a déja vu experience? You find yourself passing by a venue feeling you've been this way before; walking through a crowd and looking at the faces, many of which seem too familiar. They are part of a distant memory from a sordid past. As you listen to other women discuss their sexual appetites, which may include masturbation, pornography, 900 numbers, multiple sex partners, and much more, you realize that their stories could be your own.

As we listened, we could feel her pain. We knew oh too well the agony of bondage, the feeling of defeat, the downward spiral of destruction. We also knew the gift of grace that God has given. He showered us in a love that was our soul's desire. As we bask in the presence of that love, we can always run to Him in order to experience victory. Praise God that He allowed our paths to cross with Kathy's and with yours (the reader), so that we can share what we know first hand about God's love and compassion for those who are struggling with sexual sin.

CHAPTER ONE
Appetite for Addiction

FEED ME – THE CRY OF ADDICTION

The baby is crying at the top of her lungs, screaming as loudly as she can for attention, "I WANT WHAT I WANT, NOW!" These are not the cries of a baby when he or she is uncomfortable. In those cries one would almost hear the child verbalize, "*Hey, I'm wet... I'm sleepy... could somebody pick me up please?*" No, this baby's cries are much more intense and urgent. These sounds, like hunger pangs, are the cries that one associates with pain. What was she hungry for—food, drugs, more attention? What did the infant need, or more importantly, want? Whether the appetite was for milk, crack, or alcohol, her appetite screamed, "Feed me, now!"

Babies, adults, our human society—we are all driven by our appetites. Whether the appetite is for money, power, sex, or life itself, these appetites clamor to be fed. Whether the needs are moral or immoral, right or wrong, is not the issue—the feeding of these appetites is the only thing that really matters.

Once that is established, then one can ask the important question: what is the true appetite that is crying out?

7

When people are hungry for something or someone, their goal is to remove that hunger pain or appetite—to feed the need—by any means necessary. This is human nature—we all have a desire to be fed. There are basic needs we want to have met — the need for attention, affection, acceptance, affirmation and affiliation. When there is a void or emptiness in any of the aforementioned areas, we seek to satisfy the resulting grumbling within.

And while we will always have unmet needs, a personal relationship with Christ will abate or even satisfy some of our needs. Augustine spoke to this when he said "[hu] man is restless and will find no rest until he rests in Christ." So there are needs that we will always have, but there are ways to live victoriously and not have our needs conqueror us.

This concept of feeding our hunger involves a physiological and biological need that all humans experience. Our brain responds to a specific area of the body, which is saying, "I'm hungry, feed me NOW."

Our brain is an incredibly powerful system. There are several specific groups of nerve cells in the brain involved in the production of the sensation of pleasure that tell the brain, "That was a good thing." Once the brain (physiological) sends out a signal to our body (biological), our needs must be met in order for the brain to stop sending the signals. It's like the desire for ice cream on a hot summer day; for a cup of coffee the first thing in the morning; for an ounce of white powder after a long day at work; or the heightened smell of a woman and man during foreplay before they enjoy a sexual encounter.

The danger occurs when the need turns into a compulsive desire in which the person has lost control and becomes powerless to make healthy choices. The person has lost willpower and can no longer resist. That need is now affecting and eventually controlling their choices. Unmet needs can eventually result in appetites that affect human behavior.

At the age of fourteen, Brenda developed a relentless appetite for feeling good mentally, emotionally and physically. She had lost her father at age 11. Brenda's hunger pangs for encouragement, love, and feeling that she was special to someone, had not been fed for three years. She was starving. There were others in her life nurturing her, but it was not the same as being with her father. It didn't really seem to soothe her where she really needed soothing. He had made her world safe and secure. His encouragement and the appropriate behaviors he modeled taught Brenda how to have her needs met in a healthy way. He had been developing her character through his own integrity and as a servant to the community. Every time she looked at him she was proud and pleased that he was her father. In those pre-teen years, Brenda's identity was starting to formulate.

Early one morning Brenda's mother woke her and shared the devastating news that her father had died. She immediately went into denial. She distanced herself from the rest of her family so she would not have to share her emotional hurts or risk being hurt again by loving anyone else who might die on her.

Brenda started smoking marijuana on a whim, and it satisfied her hunger pains for a while. She didn't want to admit that a part of her identity atrophied due to the loss of her father. Getting high gave her a false sense of confidence, control, and courage. Little did Brenda know that her body was setting up tolerance levels. She soon found that she needed to smoke more marijuana, just to maintain the same intensity to feed her hunger adequately and reach her usual "feel good" level.

Tolerance is the phenomenon of always wanting or needing more of the addictive behavior, substance, or the object of attachment in order to feel satisfied. Brenda's smoking of marijuana moved from a bad habit to an addictive behavior. It had become the surrogate to fill the need to feel good mentally, emotionally, and physically as well as building her self-esteem. On the contrary, the more of the drug she used, the lower her self-esteem became. She not only increased her intake of marijuana but also obtained a stronger form of the drug, the marijuana called "red bud." Her body adjusted to each new level and the cycle continued to grow. Brenda added new and different drugs to compensate for her desire to feel better and gain more self-assurance.

Eventually, Brenda discovered alcohol. Alcohol was easily accessible and less expensive and had a different stimulus effect and attachment of control. Have you ever seen a teenager operate under the influence of alcohol, assuming all the while they are in full control? It's like going to a play. The stage is set and the teen is the star attraction in complete control of her audience and in demand by all. This was Brenda's world. Alcohol infused volumes of false confidence into Brenda's low self-esteem. She thought she had found the solution to her poor self-image—Cognac, strong yet smooth liquor. Brenda eventually started having "yak (cognac) attacks." She believed this was the pivotal point of addiction in her life because, for Brenda, drinking alcohol had become a prerequisite for feeling happy.

The cycle of addictive behavior caused her to continually try something new and different, in the hopes that this new thing would do the trick in making her feel good about herself. Whatever was the "in thing" to make her feel good, she tried. Prompted by her peer's immoral worldview and society through commercials and other media, she was attached to drugs and alcohol. Brenda thought they fulfilled her needs and made up for what she had lost when her father died. They certainly helped to dull her pain and other emotions surrounding his death. This is the underlying process that re-sults in addictive behavior—attaching to something that you desire to replace something you feel you have lost. *Prone to wander, Lord I feel it. Prone to leave the God I love. Here's my heart, O take and seal it. Seal it for Thy courts above.*

Brenda's sexual addiction arrived on the scene before her drug use began. She was promiscuous at a young age. She wanted desperately to be loved. She wanted attention and af-fection. Like many teenagers she confused sex with love. She wanted to be touched. As a child she had discovered the pleasures of touching herself. She became entrapped in the act of masturbation and developed an appetite for the feelings associated with it. When stimulating herself was no longer satisfying, she heightened the sexual sensation with multiple objects and longer durations. She wanted more. Even giving her body to whoever was willing did not satisfy. Yes, she was feeling good and "getting off" but it left her feeling empty and guilty. She then needed to do something to ease her pain. Sex, along with her other addictions had been her answer. One of the many dangers of sexual sin is that it may start off as a si-lent, hidden sin but it progresses. As the person wakes up from all the pain, they discover that what they have is more than a bad habit — it's a full-blown addiction. Brenda's ad-diction provided some temporary comfort but it did not meet the need or address the longing in her soul.

CHAPTER TWO
More Than a Bad Habit

SEXUAL ADDICTION – WHAT IS IT?

According to Gerald May in his book, *Addiction and Grace*, "Addiction is any compulsive, habitual behavior that limits the freedom of human desire." In other words, it narrows the choices or alternatives for the outlet of those desires. The term "behavior" indicates that action is essential to addiction. Those actions become habits and before long the habit is driving the attitude. The attitude believes that the actions being exhibited are rational and normal, but nothing is further from the truth.

Gerald May also indicates that virtually anything in life can become an object of attachment (habit). It is especially important to remember however, that there is a vast difference between having strong feelings about something and being addicted to it. That difference is freedom. Addictions are compulsive habitual behaviors that engulf and compromise our freedom. They tend to take on a personality of their own. The addiction is the driving force behind the behavior. Addictions come in many forms.

13

In addition to the **attraction addictions** (those things that we are compelled to do or drawn to), there are also **aversion addictions**. Simply stated, an aversion addiction is an attraction addiction in reverse. The best example of this is racial, ethnic, or sexual prejudices, and phobias. Instead of tolerance, where the victim can't get enough of something, they experience intolerance. No matter how little of something they have, it is still too much. Instead of withdrawal symptoms, the distress they experience when they lose something results in feelings of panic, fear, or disgust when the victim gets too close to that which they abhor (May, 1989).

Chart #1

Attraction Addictions			Aversion Addictions		
Anger	Exercise	Nail biting	Airplanes	Death	Needles
Approval	Fame	Relationships	Anchovies	Dentists	Open
Chocolate	Gambling	Scab picking	Anger	Dirt	space
Cleanliness	Golf	Sex	Animals	Doctors	Pain
Coffee	Gossiping	Shoplifting	Blood	Embarrassment	Public
Competition	Guilt	Sleeping	Bridges	Failure	Sex
Contest	Hair	Sports	Closed space	Fire	Speaking
Drinking	twisting	Stress	Commitment	Germs	Rejection
Drugs	Idolatry	Television	Conflict	High places	Storms
Eating	Messiness	Tobacco	Crowds	Intimacy	Test
Envy	Movies	Work	Darkness	Loneliness	Traffic
					Tunnels

(Adapted from Gerald Mays, Addiction & Grace, 1989)

The general definition of addiction is a state of compulsion, obsession, or pre-occupation that enslaves a person's will and desire. Addiction sidetracks and eclipses the energy of a person's deepest, truest desires for love and goodness.

Sexual Addiction is not a household word, yet it's a worldwide affliction. People who are addicted to sex are individuals who are out of control and have lost their ability to say no. Their sexual behavior has become a continuous downward spiral. Sex has ceased to be a source of pleasure for them, but is actually a reality of pain. This person relies on sex for escape, comfort from pain, or relief from stress, but is not limited to these avenues of release. The compulsivity is the primary focus in the person's life, and they ignore other things and people who are important, such as family, friends, and work—in short, everything. They will even compromise their own values and standards.

According to professionals who work in this field, sexually compulsive behavior has reached epidemic proportions. The National Council on Sexual Addiction Compulsivity estimated that 6 to 8% of Americans are sex addicts. That relates to approximately 16 to 21.5 million people (Amparano, 1998). The National Council on Sexual Addiction and Compulsivity has defined sexual addiction as *"persistent and escalating patterns of sexual behavior acted out despite increasing negative consequences to self and others."* Sex is a drug for millions of people who are attempting to deaden their pain. The pain can have many faces: loneliness, child abuse, low self-esteem, fear of failure, fear of success, pride...the list may be endless.

As a single woman, Charlotte has a desire for a life mate chosen by God. Time does not seem to be on her side. There are some nights when the struggle with loneliness is unbearable. Many women in the church wake up daily to this scenario after suffering through a long night. However, Charlotte has learned the hard way that fantasy and masturbation only complicate and prolong the struggle. Inordinate attachment to the opposite sex or same sex at times has come easier than waiting for a life mate. Being hungry for affection and attention has led down a path of sexual sin.

Women who struggle with sexual sin and/or addiction may be sitting next to you in the pew. People with sexual addictions are not just the perverts in office jokes. They are some of the respectable people you know: corporate executives, doctors, lawyers, preachers, presidents, deacons, neighbors, and our family members. They are often the people you least expect, including yourself. Consider these statistics on the background profile of the typical person with sexual addiction: 81% report being sexually abused during their childhood, 73% report being physically abused, and 97% were emotionally abused and /or neglected as children. Some statistics of their educational and socioeconomic status are as follows: 42% of the people earn more than $30,000 a year, 58% are college graduates, and 65% are professional people with second degrees and/or graduate degrees (National Coalition for the Protection of Children & Families, 1999). Those struggling or addicted to sex are not some man or woman in the back alley. They are all of us living out the desire for eternity; God-given gifts gone awry: pursuit of heaven here (i.e. false expectations)—you and I—living double lives of pain and pleasure.

What are some indicators of addictive sexual behavior? The first indicator is that addictive sex is done in isolation. It is secretive, devoid of intimacy, and separate from relationships. Addictive sex victimizes and it ends in despair. This type of secretive and isolated behavior is a signal that something is wrong, very wrong. When we say addictive sex is done in isolation, it doesn't necessarily mean that it is done when the person is physically alone, but it can mean that. It can also mean that the person is emotionally detached from the experience; their involvement in the sexual act is in the third person. When someone is struggling with sexual addiction, they may be involved physically, but their thoughts and emotions are outside of the experience. Just the opposite happens in intimate relationships.

The sexual act should draw us closer together in our minds and bodies, including our emotions, with all coming together in that intimate experience. The addicted person's behavior is actually secretive to the point that they can and actually do lead a double lifestyle. When the person is in their acting out behavior (addiction), he or she behaves as differently from their "normal" behavior and lifestyle as night and day. When we "act out" or do things without thinking, this behavior is a part of the private world in which you are emotionally detached. In the perceived world (non-addictive), they can be emotionally attached. At this point two personas develop: an addictive lifestyle (private) and a perceived lifestyle (public).

Mildred had this type of personality. A transformation took place as she left her public world and stepped into her private arena. As a Christian woman she epitomized being a faithful steward, warm, loving, always giving of herself. No one in her public world knew the demons she fought in her private world; a major struggle with sexual sin. It was hard living a double life but even harder experiencing the shame and guilt after each encounter. As time passed by, the conviction of the Holy Spirit waned. She was not only emotionally detached from her sexual experiences but spiritually numb as well due to her entrapment. Was it worth it? NO! Did she want out? YES! Was the pain unbearable? Absolutely. But she chose to try to ignore it and go on with her double life.

The goal of those who are addicted to sex is to mask their pain. However, as they are masking their pain, they are building up a tolerance for their present level of sexual gratification and developing an appetite for more. At the forefront of the addicted person's mind is a pre-occupation with how and when they can next feed their desire. As their desire increases, their ability to say no is paralyzed. Lack of control is the result of their need's entrapment.

Once a woman's mind enters into an agenda through fantasy, she is well on her way into sexual sin, which can lead to addiction. The impact of fantasy and thought life should not be overlooked.

CYCLES OF ADDICTIONS

As Mandy rose from bed early one morning, she contemplated what she was going to eat that day, knowing it would not be from the dinner plate. Her mind had already started working overtime in anticipation of the upcoming weekend—a planned three-day trip out of town. For a person struggling with sexual sin, which has led to addiction, the fantasy and foreplay leading up to the actual act of sexual encounter is an orgasm in itself.

The phone rang and Mandy felt an immediate rush. Dopamine filled her brain and body at the excitement of her partner's call. Words were exchanged as to where to meet and all the things that were already planned. She and her partner had just tried figuratively to kill each other sexually a few days prior, but the need for sex was as strong if not stronger today than yesterday. Mandy couldn't wait and nothing was going to get in the way of allowing her fantasy to run rampant until it couldn't run any more. Anything less than carrying out her present appetite would send her into deep despair or on the hunt for another outlet. Sexual addiction has many outlets. However, at this stage of her addiction, Mandy really did not want to make other choices because she thought she had acquired a little bit of heaven with her present partners.

The sexual addiction cycle basically consists of four

components: preoccupation, ritualization, compulsive sexual behavior, and the level of despair. This cycle is part of a larger addictive system.

Diagram #1 — The Addictive Cycle

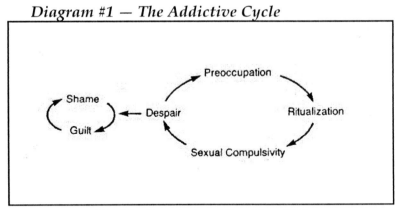

Used by Permission: Hazelden 1989

Preoccupation occurs when the mind is completely engrossed with thoughts of sex. This mental state creates an obsessive search for sexual stimulation, no matter what that acting out behavior may include. It is so consuming that it can render the addicted person nonfunctional. They will eventually become impaired emotionally, mentally, occupationally, and financially. Sexual addiction is a life-dominating sin because it has the ability to impact every area of the person's life, if allowed to continue unchecked.

The ritualization involved in sexual addiction is a special routine that leads up to the sexual acting out behavior. The ritual intensifies the preoccupation and adds to the arousal or the excitement. The person who is prone to wander starts planning when they wake up in the morning what they're going to do that afternoon. They plan on Monday what they're going to do on Saturday. Visualizing the acting out behavior intensifies the excitement for them. It's the buildup, the preoccupation, and the mindset that feeds their need, which is why their minds must constantly be renewed.

When sex addicts finish acting out their ritual, the gratification is followed by a disappointing empty void. There is an immediate rush, a gratification that lasts for a brief time. But when it is over the person wonders, "Is that it? I've been planning this, I've been waiting for this, looking forward to this, I get it, and it's over?!"   The addicted person is then overwhelmed with guilt and shame. He or she is left at the point of despair—feeling utterly hopeless, helpless, and worthless about his or her powerlessness over his or her behavior.

The third component in the addictive cycle, "sexual compulsivity, is the inability to control one's sexual behavior. This compulsive behavior is the cornerstone of the addiction. To be preoccupied and to ritualize are precursors to this stage; but without the acting out, the addiction is not established, because the behavior is still under control." (Carnes, *Contrary to Love*, pg. 65) There's a moment that comes for every addict, when the consequences are so great and the pain is so bad, that they will finally admit that their life is out of control because of that sexual behavior.

After a sexual act, the person in bondage will feel the effects of a downward spiral that represents their emotions of despair and shame. It creates a feeling of emptiness and guilt with the realization that they are powerless against this trapped feeling of sexual desire. In an effort to feel healthy and whole again or at least have a balanced feeling of, "I'm not a bad person, I'm all right," they repeat the cycle again. The sole purpose of the cycle is to mask the pain. Addicts will even participate in the cycle to mask the pain originally created by participating in the cycle.

Diagram #2 – The Addictive System

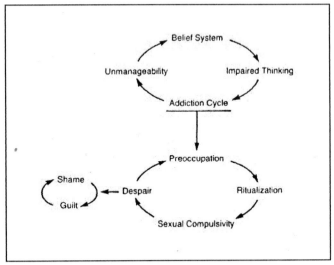

Used by Permission: Hazelden 1989

Parallel to the cycle of addictions is an addictive system. Just as the addictive cycle is self-perpetuating, the larger addictive system kicks in to reinforce itself. The four component subsystems of the addictive system are the belief system, impaired thinking, unmanageability, and the addictive cycle (Carnes, 1989). We equate the belief system involved in an addictive system to the belief system used in the Garden of Eden. Eve believed a lie as though it was the truth, and so the enemy beguiled her. The person who is prone to wander has a belief system that operates in the same way; they are beguiled.

A psychologist might use the term "cognitive dissonance" to describe the battle inside a person who believes one way and acts another, and might well describe their behavior as incongruent with their statements. For example, a woman will normally feel intense cognitive dissonance if she secretly carries on an affair with another man while pretending to be happily married to her husband. Others say she should be happy in her marriage, but she doesn't feel that way even if she says that she does. She is living out her sexual compulsion with various outlets other than her marital relationship. One important indication of faulty beliefs is evident when the addiction increases the person's negative feelings about him or herself. When exhibiting the out of control behavior, the person interprets it to mean, "I am a bad, unworthy person."

Flowing out of the faulty belief system is impaired thinking, which usually involves a distortion of reality. Types of impaired thinking include denial, rationalization, self-delusion, self-righteousness, and/or blaming others. Remember Eve in the Garden of Eden? Her thinking patterns were obviously impaired. The person experiencing impaired thinking violates such personally held values as honesty and/or fidelity. Procrastination and low productivity at work may compound their difficulties. What the individual believes is rational is actually the opposite.

The person constantly justifies him or herself by saying, "My addiction is under control. I can stop whenever I want to." But this usually occurs after the next encounter. They will try to cover their behavior through denial, procrastination, lies, and alienation from their family and the real (perceived) world. What results could be compared to a cat unraveling a ball of string—a big tangled-almost impossible-to-unravel-mess. Fueled by shame and guilt, The Addictive System feeds into The Addictive Cycle. The addict's life becomes unmanageable. In the beginning, the person has an addiction, and in the end, the addiction has them.

In God's Word we find hope, help, and healing for everyone in bondage to addiction. *Romans 12:1-2 states, "I urge you brothers/sisters, in view of God's mercy, to offer your bodies as living sacrifices, holy and pleasing to God. This is your spiritual act of worship. Do not conform any longer to the pattern of this world, but be transformed by the renewing of your mind. Then you will be able to test and approve what God's will is, His good, pleasing and perfect will."*

Our belief system and impaired thinking must be changed and renewed. We don't want to be unstable and double-minded (James 1:8). As a man thinks, so goes his action. Ephesians 4:22-24 holds the key to break the addictive system. *"You were taught, with regard to your former way of life, to put off your old self, which is being corrupted by its deceitful desires, to be made new in the attitude of your minds, and to put on the new self, created to be like God in true righteousness and holiness."*

Any time we stop a behavior we need to replace the old behavior with a new one. Replace it with a behavior that will build us up or encourage us as women who know God. Look for something that will draw you closer to God and His Word. If I put off calling my sex partner, then I need to put on calling a believer in Christ who does not have a character that is "prone to wander." My put on is accountability to that other person. Do two walk together unless they have agreed to do so? Have you agreed with someone? Have you linked with an accountability partner who knows the level of your struggle with sexual sin?

LEVELS OF ADDICTION

As the person who is prone to wander continues to act out the addiction, they escalate into certain areas of behavior that they believe will better meet their needs. This is a perfect demonstration of the progression of sin. We read in Romans that there is a progression of sin as the dark side of our desire continues to be fed. While sin and desire are progressive, societal norms, laws, or fear can all prevent a person's level of addiction from escalating. Initially introduced by Patrick Carnes, Ph.D. in the early 80's, there was conceptualized three levels of addictions. Dr. Carnes' insight has helped to heal many sexually addicted individuals. At the end of this century, we have noted other levels of addiction, along with Carnes' (1983) three foundational levels.

Level One includes behavior that is perceived in our culture as acceptable. The reality is that widespread practice conveys a public tolerance. These practices include masturbation, multiple heterosexual and homosexual relationships, pornography, and prostitution.

Level Two specifies sexual behavior that is generally regarded as nuisance behavior. These behaviors include exhibitionism, voyeurism, tranvestism, bestiality, indecent phone calls, and indecent liberties (pretending to accidentally brush up against others in public places).

Level Three includes sexual behaviors that are dangerous, abusive, or life threatening. They include incest, child molestation, sexual abuse of vulnerable adults, and rape.

Level four includes sexual activity via virtual reality, simulcasting, webcams, etc.

Level five includes sex coupled with violence and aggression often leading to death.

Levels four and five are proposed by the authors of this text and are currently being researched. There is not necessarily a specific order to the addicted person's progression from level one to level five. Their order of progression depends on the individual's appetite. Lust fuels the addict's appetite and is at the core of the addict's palate.

The road to recovery starts with admitting that you are powerless in the face of this all-encompassing appetite and acknowledging that God is all-powerful. God is our strong tower. We can run, even from the stronghold of sexual addiction, to Him to be saved.

The concept here is to run. Joseph ran from Potiphar's wife as she tried to lure him into a sexual encounter. As we run from sexual sin we must run toward a specific place (God's strong tower). He is the only one who can bind the strongman.

THE DARK SIDE OF DESIRE

The dark side of desire is the struggle within, which leads the person to act out in ways that are contrary to the biblical standards set forth in the Word of God. In this struggle, the ultimate result is sin that directly separates us from God. The problem goes back to the Garden of Eden when the serpent posed the question to Eve,

> *"Did God really say you must not eat from any tree in the garden?" Eve replied, "We may eat fruit from the trees in the garden, but God did say we must not eat fruit from the tree that is in the middle of the garden, and we must not touch it, or we will die." "You will not surely die," the serpent said to the woman. "For God knows that when you eat of it your eyes will be opened, and you will be like God, knowing good and evil." (Genesis 3:2-5)*

Good and evil have been present since the creation of the world. The turning point was when Eve made *a decision, a choice to obtain and taste of something that was forbidden.* This one act exposed all of humanity to an appetite for sin – the forbidden. The dark side is innate, a latent behavior within all of us. Yet we have the ability granted by God to chose between good and evil.

The dark side of desire has been around since the Fall of Man. *In Genesis 3: 8-11: "Then the man and his wife heard the sound of the Lord God as He was walking in the garden in the cool of the day, and they hid from the Lord God among the trees of the garden. But the Lord God called to the man, Where are you? He answered, I heard you in the garden, and I was afraid because I was naked; so I hid. And He said who told you that you were naked? Have you eaten from the tree that I commanded you not to eat from?"*

God had set the standard regarding which trees to eat from and He had given a command. Due to the disobedience of the first man and woman, a side within them was awakened—the dark side of desire—which then turned into an appetite of pride and selfishness. The dark side of desire is me-focused: my desires, my wants, and my needs without regard to others. We all have a dark side as a result of sin. The end result could be as described in Romans 1:18-32.

> *The wrath of God is being revealed from heaven against all the Godlessness and wickedness of men who suppress the truth by their wickedness, since what may be known about God is plain to them because God has made it plain to them. For since the creation of the world, God's invisible qualities, His eternal power and divine nature, have been clearly seen. These invisible qualities have been understood from what has been made and have been observed in nature as well so that men are without excuse. For although they knew God, they neither glorified him as God nor gave thanks to Him, but their thinking be-*

came futile and their foolish hearts were darkened. Although they claimed to be wise, they became fools and exchanged the glory of the immortal God for images made to look like mortal man and birds and animals and reptiles. Therefore God gave them over to the sinful desires of their hearts, including sexual impurity for the degrading of their bodies with one another. They exchanged the truth of God for a lie, and worshipped and served created things rather than the Creator, who is forever to be praised, Amen. Because of this, God gave them over to shameful lusts. Even their women exchanged natural relations for unnatural ones. In the same way the men also abandoned natural relations with women and were inflamed with lust for one another. Men committed indecent acts with other men, and received in themselves the due penalty for their perversion. Furthermore, since they did not think it worthwhile to retain the knowledge of God, He gave them over to a depraved mind, to do what ought not to be done. They have become filled with every kind of wickedness, evil, greed and depravity. They are full of envy, murder, strife, deceit and malice. They are gossips, slanderers, God-haters, insolent, arrogant and boastful. They invent ways of doing evil; they disobey their parents; they are senseless, faithless, heartless, and ruthless. Although they know God's righteous decree, that those who do such things deserve death, they not only continue to do these very things but also approve of those who practice them.

As a little girl seven years old, Debra asked her mother, "Where do babies come from?" Her mother had recently brought her little brother home from the hospital. She gave Debra a detailed description of sex but in words Debra could understand. This left a strange impression on Debra's young mind. She realized, as a result of a man and a woman having sex, that there was a strong possibility a baby would be the result. She didn't want to have a baby anytime soon but she wanted to have a sexual experience. Her mother's detailed description triggered increased curiosity and even created some premature excitement about the feeling of having sex. The Bible warns in the book of Solomon to not awaken desire before it's time (2:7b).

When Debra was ten years old, one of her female cousins (14 years old) molested her. Debra knew that what was happening to her was wrong, but she complied due to threats of exposure. It happened during a family reunion one summer night. Debra and her cousin shared a bed together as the families chipped in to put everyone up for the weekend. She remembered feeling these exciting sensations all over her body. Her cousin told her to be quiet and that she would make her feel real special. So she lay there thinking how special she felt and that it was her same sex cousin so she knew she could not get pregnant. As the night went on Debra recalled that the sex play was scary at first but became enjoyable and exciting. It was an experience that she wanted to repeat.

She was confused, as well as overwhelmed with guilt and shame. Yet, she found herself not only having sex play with her cousin but also exploring other young girls who also found the feeling strangely exciting. Debra used the same coercion tactics with her victims as those that were used with her. She even embellished what she told them to be more convincing and to ensure their silence. Her mind was bombarded with negative emotions. But to her dismay, she could not help herself and continued to satisfy her feelings. Debra's dark side was awakened by the unfortunate act of molestation.

Dark desires can be awakened by various means. The following statistics taken from a national survey conducted by Patrick Carnes, of 600 recovering sex addicts represent the impact of family dynamics on the development of sexual addiction and lifestyle choices.

Family of origin
* 72% come from severely dysfunctional families
* 87% have another addiction of some type in the family

Victimization
* 97% were emotionally abused
* 81% were sexually abused
* 73% were physically abused

An individual like Debra can be a sexual victim or have sexual thoughts and fantasies from watching behavior through various media (discussed more in Chapter 3). Even when the dark side is awakened prematurely, there is still hope, help, and healing available. We have a choice and a responsibility to confess, confront and control the dark side.

Debra's story, like so many others, is tragic. Yet there is hope, although it is a painful process towards healing. The bondage is dismantled when the silence that has kept us captive is broken.

While speaking at a conference on sexual deviancy, the Spirit of God was upon me and I (Sabrina) shared some of my story. My personal testimony of bondage struck a cord with many in the audience who were still in captivity. This group of walking wounded (many of whom had not been healed) connected with various points of my journey. Many had been delivered from the memories of abuse and/or addiction but had not overcome the guilt of what they had done or what had been done to them and the shame of who they perceived themselves to be as a result. The impact of guilt and shame rendered many ineffective in their witness and in their walk with God.

As we help to open up windows of hope, help, and healing for the reader, our clients, colleagues, and others, our mission is to be transparent about what God has done in our lives. There are so many that the Lord has set free, but they are not willing to tell their story.

The cost of breaking the silence as well as the overwhelming guilt and shame regarding their past still has them bound. If God has delivered us from bondage, we should be able to stand up and tell someone. There are those who are still caught up and they are looking for someone with whom they can be honest—someone who can truly empathize. When clients come in for counseling to talk about their addictive lifestyles, we know exactly what they are talking about because we've been there. Best of all, God's presence in our lives is a constant reminder that we have been forgiven through the work of Jesus Christ.

Sexual addiction is an all consuming lifestyle. It is a relationship with sex, devoid of intimacy, marked by five central characteristics of addiction: tolerance, which we have already discussed, withdrawal, self-deception, loss of will power, and distortion of attention.

A person who is experiencing withdrawal, who desires to walk away from the lifestyle, will be impacted in their physical bodies—and the impact is emotional and mental. Walking away from the addiction is an impossible task when we are trying to do it in our own energy and strength. Paul talked about this struggle in Romans chapter 7. He indicated that the good that he could do, he didn't do. And the very evil that he knew not to do, he continued to find himself doing. As he struggled with withdrawing from a life of sin, he asked a very important question, "Who shall deliver me from this body of death?" The answer: "Thanks be to God through Jesus Christ."

Paul realized that he needed the power of God in order to overcome his battle with the flesh. Who are you relying on to fight the battles of your flesh? Take the first step – admit you are powerless and acknowledge your need for God.

For those who remain in the addiction, their denial is manifested in the self-deception that they are victims. They rationalize, minimize, and justify the behavior because of a warped perspective of reality. They are in denial to themselves that their lifestyle really is a problem. Denial is a defense mechanism of self-medication. If I continue to deny my addiction, it will become a part of who I believe I am. For example struggling with masturbation, fornication, and pornography can be an overwhelming experience. But it doesn't help us if we pretend these struggles don't exist. We need to face our problems and work to overcome them.

As a single woman struggling with the desire to feel stimulated at times, I (LaVern) found myself caught up in self-masturbation. I knew that sex was to take place between a husband and a wife. My rationale was, it's just me and I'm not having sex with anyone else. How could this be sinful? I found myself masturbating often and fantasizing more and more. It reached a point where I was not able to stop or just say no. My body wanted this stimulation and more. My rationalization was, "This is not hurting anyone." I was the one it hurt and found myself addicted to level 1 of the Carnes model. Self-sex is devoid of intimacy, done in isolation, and separate from relationships. I (LaVern) was caught up and setting myself up for a roller coaster ride toward pornography.

Women may realize that various activities are bad, but they are bombarded each day by deviance that our society accepts and promotes as normal. Irrational thoughts (sick perceptions) become reality and addiction becomes rational.

The absence of will power, self-control, or self-discipline, characterized by the inability to stop the addiction is the point where the person finally realizes he/she needs help. Their addiction has become a god in their life. Addiction is an idolatrous lifestyle because something else has replaced the reality of God in the person's life. The person has been captured and kept in bondage. Praise God that Jesus came to set the captives free. At this stage, they have often fallen into a pit so deep that it is difficult to climb out without the help of a professional counselor who is directed and assisted by the Wonderful Counselor (Isaiah 9:6b).

The greatest fear of a person in sexual bondage is that they will be found out—EXPOSED. Ironically, the greatest way to experience relief is to be exposed. James encourages us, *"to confess our faults, one to another that we may be healed"* (James 5:16). The accuser of the brethren (your enemy, the devil) will always haunt you with the belief that you will be destroyed when the truth is discovered. Those with sexual addictions believe their will power (which they do not realize has already been lost), will enable them to quit when they are good and ready. The false belief system says, "If I quit now, while nobody knows, I don't have to confess anything." When they are unable to succeed, they are plunged into an abyss of despair. And they learn that one quick cure for despair is to act out sexually (converting emotional response to behavior with the absence of logic).

Imagine how difficult that must be! If their greatest fear is that they are going to be found out, then how do they seek help? This seems to be a no-win situation. The internal conflict alone is binding enough. A crossroads for sex addicts occurs when they wonder, "Is there someone out there who is safe, somewhere I can go to share my shame, guilt, despair and sin?" Remember, in order to seek help, the addict needs to move forward and tell someone. *Prone to wander, Lord, I feel it. Prone to leave the God I love. Here's my heart. O take and seal it. Seal it for Thy courts above.*

CHAPTER THREE
Subliminal Seduction

EASILY SEDUCED

Falling into sexual sin is easier than you think. As we explore together the different media through which people become entangled you may see yourself. These avenues leading to sexual sin allow individuals to be anyone and everyone they choose to be at anytime almost anywhere. The anonymity involved provides the opportunity for those who are prone to wander to venture into sin without immediate exposure.

In the 80's, the theaters engaged in a marketing program that flashed certain products on the movie screen. The images would not last long enough for you to actually recognize the details of the product. This marketing strategy was called subliminal imaging. The most prevalent areas where those struggling with sexual sin and addiction are subliminally seduced include fantasies, movies, and television. Fantasies offer us a porthole to go anywhere we want to go without others knowing. Movies are a way we can look at others engaging in sexual sin from heterosexual to homosexual activity. Television brings sexual sin into the comfort of your home through soft porn during the daytime soap operas to R-rated viewing in prime time.

PORTHOLES OF PASSION: FANTASY

A porthole is a type of window on a boat that allows light to shine in and air to flow through. In moving forward to seek help, the addicted person finds herself looking through a porthole. However, not the one that leads to freedom. Her imaginary porthole is a "fantasy." She believes that she is in total control of her destinations and can depart from any-where imaginable and arrive free of charge. Initially, the ad-dicted person believes there is no cost. That would be the trip of a lifetime—free to go anywhere you can imagine.

This belief is due in part to the fact no one else knows the addicted person is traveling. Portholes can take the indi-vidual to any destination she desires at any time of the day or night. These love boat fantasy cruises are never overbooked, because she believes she is the only one traveling. The fantasy life is so intriguing. Yet an insightful therapist, professional counselor, or trained pastor can use the person's cognitive distortion as an indicator of the level of addiction at which the addict is operating.

Manipulation begins with our thought life, and in-volves how we think and process information. Our fantasy life also has similarities to Eve in the Garden of Eden when she started communicating with the serpent about who she was and what she could become (verbal daydreaming). Go back and take a look at the conversation that was going on between the serpent and Eve in *Genesis 3:1b-5, he asks, "Did God really say you must not eat from any tree in the garden?"* The conversation that Eve had with the serpent often times depicts the sex addict's fantasy life. It is a belief that what we imagine in our minds is in some way true or real. In its essence, a fantasy is an unreal mental image, illusion, or a daydream.

The serpent took God's truth and inserted doubt. This is beguilement: believing a lie as if it is truth. In *Genesis 2:16-17, God stated, "You are free to eat from any tree in the garden; but you must not eat from the tree of the knowledge of good and evil, for when you eat of it you will surely die."* The serpent injected doubt by questioning Eve's freedom of choice, and then telling her she was not going to die. When we operate in sin, death is always the by-product. Eve was deceived and did not, perhaps could not, discern that the death was spiritual not physical. The serpent made his lie attractive by telling Eve she could be like God. *"... For God knows that when you eat of it your eyes will be opened, and you will be like God, knowing good and evil."* *This was the serpent's own desire and the reason he was cast from heaven—he wanted to become like the Most High (Isaiah 14:12-14).*

Eve may have been fantasizing about her role as a woman on the earth, thinking she and Adam had more coming to them than what God had already presented. He gave Adam dominion and authority over the earth, but perhaps God was holding out on them. Eve's doubt of not having all she deserved opened the door to a fantasy of beguilement that in turn led to her spiritual death. But, as in everything, God had made provision for the imminent fall. *"Just as sin entered the world through one man, and death through sin, in this way death came to all men, because all have sinned" (Romans 5:12).* Because of Eve's disobedience, spiritual death was imminent. *"Just as the result of one trespass was condemnation for all men, so also the result of one act of righteousness was justification that brings life for all men. For just as through the disobedience of the one man, the many were made sinners, so also through the obedience of the one man, the many will be made righteous"* (Romans 5:18-19).

For a person addicted to sex, their fantasy life eventually reaches a point where irrational thoughts become their reality. The addicted person daydreams many times in a week, a day, or an hour. She may travel all over the city, country, and continent. In some strange distorted way, believes it's free, fun, and fulfilling. But her idle mind has become the devil's playground, and it will cost her.

In the mind of the addicted individual, a family movie can become an X-rated film, and X-rated movies seem like a family past time. An addict adds her own "story line" to the scenes being played out in the movie. Though the movie comes to an end, for the one struggling with addiction the movie continuously stays in reruns. The arena for the fantasy life is people, places, and foreplay. She can obtain a rush just by imagining past events or future encounters.

Let's set up a typical picture of a sex addict and imagine it is someone at work. Mikki bounces into the office and speaks to everyone she passes as she makes her way to her private office. Before sitting down at the computer to check e-mail and voice mail messages, she glances out her door, then closes it. The day has just begun and she has already gone into a trance and prepares to take a cruise. This is her daily ritual. In the confines of her mind, she fantasizes a sexual encounter with everyone she has spoken with in the office.

The surge of dopamine in her brain provides an intense stimulus for a sensual, sexual fantasy. Twenty minutes later she was on her way to the rest room to finish what she had started. As she returned to the office, she looked through a different porthole for more passion. We know that it is difficult to imagine that a woman's struggle with sexual sin could be this intense. But this is a reality for many women.

For some women, a simple click of the computer screen can put them into a whole world of various pornographic sites. If there is a block on the computer, they can easily take out their personal cell phone, call any one of the 900 numbers available and talk to people who will converse with them using language that will stimulate them until their next break. All the while, no one in the office has been remotely aware that the person has been on a cruise of sexual fantasy. The deception for the addicted person is to think that it didn't cost them anything, when in reality it costs time, energy, productivity, and freedom to choose. As an addict, she is powerless over her compulsivity.

God gives everyone the freedom to choose. His desire is that we choose Him, His will and His ways. Each choice we make has consequences, or rewards. We are driven by our decisions, which determine our destiny. Our position, profile, or purpose in life does not matter. Our allegiances fall prey to our choices.

In the book of Romans, the Apostle Paul makes this concept very clear, stating that we are either slaves to righteousness or slaves to sin. *"What then? Shall we sin because we are not under law but under grace? By no means! Don't you know that when you offer yourselves to someone to obey him as slaves, you are slaves to the one whom you obey whether you are slaves to sin, which leads to death, or to obedience, which leads to righteousness"* *(Romans 6:15-16)*.

Our choices will shape our lives and affect others. What we value and believe is the undercurrent that shapes our outlook on life. There are a number of philosophies in our world system that fight for our attention and allegiances. Whether it is immoral, materialistic, passion and/or pleasure, the world-systems want and solicit our membership.

The price of membership is ever increasing immorality. How did we, as a society, progress from having sex in the sanctity of a marriage in the 1950's to teenage group sex in our public schools in the 21st century? We live in a world where anything and every-thing goes. What messages is our society giving us? Are there forces or agendas behind these messages? The Bible says yes, in Ephesians 6:12: *"For our struggle is not against flesh and blood, but against the rulers, against the authorities, against the powers of this dark world and against the spiritual forces of evil in the heavenly realms."* Today there is a war being waged for our minds.

We are bombarded daily with evil and seductive philosophies including mankind's various world-views. At times the devil gives the illusion that he is winning his battle against God. Not so! We know that the war is already won by God because the victory is declared in Revelation 20:7-10. This does not mean that the old serpent, the devil, does not attempt on a daily basis to ensnare individuals into believing that they are making right choices. One of his schemes is to have us believe that there is no such thing as a bad or wrong choice. But God says for every choice we make there are consequences—some good, some bad. Remember that Eve's choice produced spiritual death and eternal consequences that affected all of humanity.

In our world today many choices exist that draw us away from God. The Bible calls these "idols." These idols can also be referred to as "isms." An ism is the condition of being, conduct or qualities characteristic of a society. They are a direct links to our portholes of passion. There are many worldly "isms." This list is in no way exhaustive, but we will discuss a few contained here and how they relate to sexual addiction.

1. **Materialism** — the most important thing in life is the ownership of possessions. Our values as an individual are based on what we own.
2. **Existentialism** — Live for the moment; it's all that you have.
3. **Individualism** — the most important person in your life is you.
4. **Hedonism** — Pleasure, happiness, and fun are the primary purposes of life.
5. **Secularism** — God is not significant. At best, He is irrelevant.
6. **Anti-historicism** — Truth is relative and not as important as being politically correct.
7. **Pragmatism** — If it works, do it.
8. **Victims** — I am the way I am because of what other people have done to me.

Materialism has always been a strong seductive porthole. Often people's self-worth is connected to their incomes and the objects that they own. These objects range from elaborate homes to owning businesses, franchises, and everything in between. The world looks at America and marvels. Even third world countries see our poor as wealthy in comparison. We live our lives striving for material gain as if it is the ultimate stamp on our identity. At times along the way, our clouded values goad our appetite to obtain more.

As we look through the porthole, we don't realize that our appetite has turned into an idol. Now we have given our allegiance and dedication to obtain more possessions at the cost of other things in our lives. For instance, we are willing to work overtime to purchase a particular item as opposed to having more time to spend with our families. Or, we have had our eyes on a piece of property and willingly sacrifice three more years until it becomes ours. Nothing is wrong with obtaining more for yourself and your family. It becomes a problem when obtaining those things takes over your life and comes between you and the Lord.

The "ism" will dictate how you invest your time, treasures, and talents. Are you living from paycheck to paycheck, in debt, living beyond your means, not tithing, not giving because you're in the red? Ask yourself, "Who is in control? Me? God, or something else?" In the book of Ecclesiastes, Solomon (the richest man who ever lived) states,

> *Whoever loves money never has money enough; whoever loves wealth is never satisfied with his income. This too is meaningless. As goods increase, so does the appetite of those who consume them. And what benefit are they to the owner except to feast his eyes on them? The sleep of a laborer is sweet, whether he eats little or much, but the abundance of a rich man permits him no sleep. I have seen a grievous evil under the sun: wealth hoarded to the harm of its owner, or wealth lost through some misfortune, so that when he has a son there is nothing left for him. Naked a man comes from his mother's womb, and as he comes, so he departs. He takes nothing from his labor that he can carry in his hand (Ecclesiastes 5:10-17).*

God says in Proverbs 30:15b-16, "*There are three things that are never satisfied, four that never say, enough! The grave, the barren womb, land, which is never satisfied with water, and fire which never says enough."*

Materialism is the acquisition of objects, and for the sexually addicted person, people are objects—they want more and more. There is no regard for the emotions or well being of the other person. People who have accumulated wealth believe that they can buy anything they want, including immorality. For example, in the movie, "Indecent Proposal" a wealthy man offers a couple one million dollars to spend the night having sex with the wife. He had money and she was another object to possess even if just overnight. Many sex addicts are looking to collect or possess something, even if only temporarily.

Consider the case of Amelia who struggled with low self-esteem and over-compensated in her job and sexual exploits. Amelia worked 60-80 hours per week at her job as a marketing representative. When she found herself exhausted, instead of watching another customer commercial she would plug in an X-rated video for relief. On the weekends she would spend hours reading steamy romantic novels. These behaviors persisted for about six months before Amelia came in for counseling. Her presenting problem was job dissatisfaction. During those six months Amelia had purchased and read over 400 books. Many of the storylines she knew by memory. In her mind, she had become many of the characters she read about.

She had also begun a collection of numbers on her database just in case she needs to make a call to someone for comfort late at night. These sexual conquests were just fantasies now, but it would only be a matter of time before she acted them out. For those caught up in sexual sin and addiction, it's all about the chase, the conquest, and the consummation—then it's on to the next object that catches their eye. The possession of things is central to the materialistic mindset.

Moreover, when God gives any man wealth and possessions, and enables him to enjoy them, then to accept his lot and be happy in his work is a gift of God. He seldom reflects on the days of his life, because God keeps him occupied with gladness of heart (Ecclesiastes 5:19-20). Only in God does life have meaning and true pleasure. Without Him nothing satisfies, but with Him we find satisfaction and enjoyment. True pleasure comes only when we acknowledge and revere God.

Hedonism operates on the pleasure principle. Happiness and fun are the primary purposes and pursuits of life. This value system seems to be a stomping ground for many of our teenagers. In some way it is connected with the belief of youth that they can and should "sow their wild oats" before they must get serious. This form of thinking is entrapment. We may get so caught up in Hedonism that 10 to 20 years of our lives have passed before we get serious. There is nothing wrong with happiness and pleasure but when they become our gods, our focus is on optimizing our senses and our feelings instead of on realizing our purpose in life.

Consider again the words of King Solomon, the wealthiest man in the world, who engaged in every pleasure under the sun:

> I thought in my heart, "Come now, I will test you with pleasure to find out what is good." But that also proved to be meaningless, "Laughter," I said, "is foolish. And what does pleasure accomplish?" (Ecclesiastes 2:1-2)

> "I undertook great projects: I built houses for myself and planted vineyards. I made gardens and parks and planted all kinds of fruit trees in them. I made reservoirs to water groves of flourishing trees. I bought male and female slaves and had other slaves who were born in my house. I also owned more herds and flocks than anyone in Jerusalem did before me. I amassed silver and gold for acquired men and women singers,

*a harem, and myself as well the delights of the heart
of man. I became greater by far than anyone in Jeru-
salem did before me. In all this my wisdom stayed
with me. I denied myself nothing my eyes desired; I
refused my heart no pleasure" (Ecclesiastes 2:4-10a).*

Sex addicts relate to King Solomon in that they deny
themselves no pleasure. They function on, "If it feels good,
let's do it." Their quest is to alleviate their pain and discom-
fort. They believe in being rewarded with pleasure. It sounds
a little like King Solomon. He did not deny himself any pleasure, as much as his eyes could see and his heart could take in.
Yet, unlike sex addicts, King Solomon realized the uselessness
of his pursuits, but he pursued nonetheless. *"My heart took delight in all my work, and this was the reward for all my labor. Yet
when I surveyed all that my hands had done and what I had toiled to
achieve, everything was meaningless, a chasing after the wind;
nothing was gained under the sun" (Ecclesiastes 2:10b-11).*

Existentialism is also clearly outlined in the book of Ecclesiastes. This philosophy says live for the moment, because
the moment is all you have. According to God's Word, man
was not born to live for the moment but to live with purpose
and vision. A sex addict lives for the here and now, with their
sole purpose being to obtain pleasure for themselves.

Clara was well aware that not every one was doing it,
even though her friend of over ten years, Rita, had been trying
to convince her that many divorced women masturbated.
Every month it was the same routine. Just before Clara's men-
strual cycle would start she would begin to feel amorous. Her
body would burn with passion. "Just do it, just do it," she
would think to herself. Clara was overwhelmed. Rita's words
would ring in her ear, "It's okay to take care of yourself sexually, and at least you are not having sex outside of marriage."

Clara reasoned, "I'm divorced, I've got to do something." So she did, but the temporary relief only increased her anxiety. A false sense of security plagued by a cycle of guilt and shame imprisoned her mind and soul.

Solomon's theme in the book of Ecclesiastes is that a life not centered on God is meaningless and without purpose. Without God, nothing will satisfy man. That is why Jesus said, *"I came to give you life, and life more abundantly."* (John 10:10b). He also said *"I am the way, the truth and the life, no one can enter into heaven except through me."* (John 14:6) Who and what are we going to choose? Our choices dictate whether or not we fall through a porthole of passion, whether that passion is for self, possessions, or other people. As Solomon reflected back on his life, he concluded: *"Now all has been heard; here is the conclusion of the matter: Fear God and keep his commandments, for this is the whole duty of man. For God will bring every deed into judgment, including every hidden thing, whether it is good or evil"* (Ecclesiastes 12:13-14).

In the book of Joshua, Joshua had assembled all the tribes of Israel together so that they could renew their covenant with God. Joshua exhorted them, *"Now fear the Lord and serve him with all faithfulness. Throw away the gods your forefathers worshipped beyond the river and in Egypt, and serve the Lord. But if serving the Lord seems undesirable to you, then choose for yourselves this day, whom you will serve, whether the gods your forefathers served beyond the river, or the gods of the Amorites, in whose land you are living. But as for me and my household, we will serve the Lord"* (Joshua 24:14-15).

It all comes back to God allowing us to choose. Choose to obey God. *"I will not let this Book of the Law depart from my mouth, I will meditate on it day and night, so that I am careful to do everything written in it"* (Joshua 1:8a). We hope to be able to say of you as Paul said of the believers in Rome,

> *But thanks be to God that, though you used to be slaves to sin, you wholeheartedly obeyed the form of teaching to which you were entrusted. You have been set free from sin and have become slaves to right-eousness. I put this in human terms, because you are weak in your natural selves. Just as you used to offer the parts of your body in slavery to impurity and to ever-increasing wickedness, so now offer them in slavery to righteousness leading to holiness." (Romans 6:19b).*

Prone to wander, Lord I feel it. Prone to leave the God I love. Here's my heart, O take and seal it. Seal it for Thy courts above.

CINEMA-IMITATING REAL LIFE

There are many portholes through which people can be subliminally seduced. The media is constantly bombarding us with sexual images on television, in movies, in magazines, on billboards, and through music. The negative impact that sensually enticing material can have on an individual's sexuality has been ignored by many. We willingly expose ourselves without regard to repercussions. The Movie Rating System of America has estimated that of the films released each month, most are rated R and contain questionable material for Christian audiences. We know that the moviemakers are not necessarily targeting the people of God, but many of us have found ourselves viewing these films.

On the following pages you will find a personal assessment titled, " Sexual Exposure in Movies." Each of the thirty-six films listed contains a theme or brief overview and an indication of the level of sexually explicit material to which viewers have been exposed. The year the film was released in the theaters and who the key stars were is also provided to help you determine if you have seen a particular film. As you review the list, circle the number next to each of the movies you have seen in the theatre, on video, or television.

Chart #2

Sexual Exposure in Movies
© 2000 Sabrina D. Black

#	YR	Movie Title	Starring	Theme (Subliminal Seduction)	Level of Sexual Exposure
1.	86	9 ½ Weeks	Mickey Rourke Kim Bassinger	An obsessive consuming affair involving torrid sexual behaviors	Level I, II
2.	90	Bad Influence	Rob Lowe James Spader	Yuppie goes down the path of sexual perversity, drug abuse, and eventually murder	Level I, II
3.	92	Basic Instincts	Michael Douglas Sharon Stone Jeanne Triplehorn	Cop gets involved with bi-sexual murder suspect and discovers many sex secrets	Level I, II
4.	83	Betrayal	Jeremy Irons Ben Kingsley Patricia Hodge	Unfolding results of an adulterous triangle among friends	Level I, II

#	YR	Movie Title	Starring	Theme *(Subliminal Seduction)*	Level of Sexual Exposure
5.	86	Blue Velvet	David Lynch Dennis Hopper Isabella Rosseleni	Dark dank sex beneath a small town murder mystery	Level I, II
6.	84	Body Double	Craig Wasson Melanie Griffith Greg Henry	Voyeur witnesses a murder and is plunged into the sleazy world of L.A. porn stars	Level I, II, V
7.	97	Booty Call	Tommy Davidson Jamie Fox Vivica Fox	Urban workers obsessed with sex	Level I, II
8.	93	Boxing Helena	Julian Sands Bill Paxton Sherilyn Fenn	Sexual obsession and decapitation	Level I
9.	71	Carnal Knowledge	Jack Nicholson Art Garfunkel Candace Bergen	Series of vignettes which chronicle the sex life of 2 friends from college to middle age	Level I, II
10.	92	Consenting Adults	Kevin Kline Kevin Spacey Mary Elizabeth-Mastrontonio	Wife swapping and murder	Level I, II, V

#	YR	Movie Title	Starring	Theme *(Subliminal Seduction)*	Level of Sexual Exposure
11.	98	Cruel Intentions	Ryan Phillipe Reece Wither-spoon	Incestuous lust, sex as revenge amongst teens The destruction of innocence	Level I, II, III
12.	92	Crying Game	Forest Whitaker William Defoe Jaye Davidson Miranda Richardson	Love, sex, and secret identity	Level I, II
13.	93	Damage	Julliete Binoche Jeremy Irons Miranda Richardson	A member of British parlia-ment becomes sexually obsessed with his son's fiancée, then plunges into an affair even more treacherous than it would seem	Level I, II, III
14.	89	Dangerous Liaisons	Michelle Pfiefer John Malkovich Glenn Close	Sex as revenge – a game of seduc-tion and emo-tional one-upmanship as others are sexu-ally exploited for relief of boredom	Level I, II, III

#	YR	Movie Title	Starring	Theme *(Sublimi-nal Seduction)*	Level of Sexual Exposure
15.	94	Disclosure	Michael Douglas Demi Moore Donald Sutherland	Role reversal and sexual harass-ment	Level I, II, III
16.	95	Don Juan DeMarco	Marlon Brando Johnny Depp Faye Dunaway	Psychologist learns lessons about sex and love from a delu-sional patient who believes that he is Don Juan	Level I
17.	94	Exotica	Don McKellar Bruce Greenwood Mia Kirschner	Psycho sexual character study of a troubled ac-countant who frequents a local strip joint	Level I, II, III
18.	78	Eyes of Laura Mars	Faye Dunaway Tommy Lee Jones Brad Dourif	Killer stalks a high fashion photographer with psychic skills whose work obsessively links sex and violence	Level I, II, III
19.	99	Eyes Wide Shut	Tom Cruise Nicole Kid-man	Exhibitionistic carnal endeavor sexual obsession	Level I, II, III, V
20.	87	Fatal Attraction	Glenn Close Michael Douglas	A one night stand who wouldn't go away: Stalking by the woman whom he scorned	Level I, II

#	YR	Movie Title	Starring	Theme *(Subliminal Seduction)*	Level of Sexual Exposure
21.	92	Final Analysis	Richard Gere Kim Bassinger Uma Thurman	A psychiatrist gets involved with a female client and her sexy sister	Level I, II
22.	99	General's Daughter	John Travolta Madeline Stowe James Conwell	Father disowns his daughter because of her past with sex and drugs	Level I, II, III, V
23.	62	Lolita	Peter Sellers Sue Lyons James Mason	Pedophile marries to be near provocative daughter	Level I, II, III
24.	99	Lolita	Jeremy Irons Miranda Richardson	Sexual obsession and subsequent seduction	Level I, II, III
25.	77	Looking for Mr. Goodbar	Tuesday Wells Richard Gere Diane Keaton	Schoolteacher looks for love in all the wrong places, including Manhattan singles bars.	Level I, II, III
26.	92	Lover (The)	Jane March Tony Leung Frederick Meininger	Lonely teenager bored with life in the convent begins a steamy affair with 30ish Chinese Aristocrat	Level I, III

#	YR	Movie Title	Starring	Theme *(Subliminal Seduction)*	Level of Sexual Exposure
27.	93	M. Butterfly	Ian Richardson Jeremy Irons John Lone	A French diplomat in communist China carries on an extended affair with a female impersonator: Psychosexual drama	Level I, II
28.	96	Mighty Aphrodite	Woody Allen Mia Sorvino	Sports writer gets curious about the mother of his adopted son and decides to explore	Level I
29.	87	Nuts	Richard Dreyfus Maureen Stapleton Barbara Streisand	A high priced prostitute driven by childhood abuse must prove herself sane before being tried for murder.	Level I, II, III
30.	75	Once is not Enough	Kirk Douglass Deborah Raffin David Jansen	Sordid sex and dirt among the 70's jet set	Level I
31.	89	Scandal	Joanne Walley-Killmer John Hurt Bridget Fonda	Famous Profumo sex scandal of the 1960's involving London cabinet member and a showgirl	Level I, II

#	YR	Movie Title	Starring	Theme *(Subliminal Seduction)*	Level of Sexual Exposure
32.	89	Sex, Lies, and Videotape	James Spader Andie McDowell Peter Gallagher	Voyeur gets caught in a love triangle with his friend's wife and his sister-in-law mistress	Level I, II
33.	93	Sliver	Sharon Stone Tom Barringer William Baldwin	Apartment manager's voyeuristic security system captures sex and murder	Level I, II
34.	51	Streetcar Named Desire	Vivian Leigh Marlon Brando Kim Hunter	A southern belle who was a prostitute and known to rely on the kindness of strangers	Level I
35.	99	Summer of Sam	John Leguizamo Mia Sirvino	A summer rampage of killing lovers (fornication)	Level I, II, III, IV, V
36.	88	Torch Song Trilogy	Harvey Fierstein Anne Bancroft Matthew Broderick	Cross dresser looking for love while coping with a histrionic mother	Level I

The column at the far right of the chart indicates the level of sexual exposure. Notice the level of sexually explicit behavior you have been exposed to for each of the movies you have circled. A brief summary of each level follows:

Levels of Addiction

Level I — Masturbation, heterosexual and homosexual relationships, pornography, and prostitution

Level II — Exhibitionism, voyeurism, indecent phone calls, and indecent liberties (pretending to accidentally brush up against others in public places).

Level III — Child molestation, incest, and rape

Level IV — Sex via virtual reality, simulcasting, webcams, etc. *currently being researched*

Level V — Sex coupled with violence and aggression often leading to death — *currently being researched*

As this list illustrates, most popular movies contain some combination of stimuli to send a sex addict quickly through the porthole of the dark side of their desire. Movies' endless flow of visual and auditory stimuli isn't the only form of media that capture the sex addict's attention. Our own dark desires lure us away. The media is not the only problem.

A percentage of believers attend fewer than 2 to 5 movies per month, and many attend far less than this. They realize that the rating system is misleading. These same believers have access to computers, VCR's, and television, where they are caught up in perusing those sexual stimuli—in the privacy of their own homes. James 1:13-15 suggests that, *"When tempted, no one should say, 'God is tempting me' for God cannot be tempted by evil, nor does he tempt any one; but each one is tempted when, by his own evil desires, he is dragged away and enticed. Then, after desire has conceived, it gives birth to sin; and sin, when it is full-grown, gives birth to death."*

Do we realize the subliminal impact the media is having on our mind, body and soul? The 1990's were truly the electronic age. The World Wide Web was born in 1992; changing the way we communicate (email), spend our money (online gambling, shopping) and the way we do business (e-commerce). It was estimated that by the year 2001, some one billion people would be connected.

Television reached 99% of the households in the U.S. with the average viewer spending seven hours a day watching "the tube." In 1996, the television industry announced a TV Parental Guideline rating system.

Chart #3

The rating system of TV Parental Guide

Rating	Audience	(V) Violence	(S) Sexual	(L) Language	(D) Dialogue
TV Y	All Children. Especially those ages 2-6	None	None	None	None
TV Y7	Directed to Older Children. Primarily age 7 and above	May include mild fantasy or comedic violence	None	None	None
TV G	General Audience. Most parents would find content suitable	Little or no violence	None	No strong language	Little or no sexual dialogue or situation
TV PG	Parental Guidance Suggested. May be unsuitable for younger children	Moderate violence	Some sexual situations	Infrequent coarse language	Some suggestive dialogue

TV 14	Parents Strongly Cautioned to exercise greater care in monitoring program	Intense violence	Intense sexual situations	Strong coarse language	Intensely suggestive dialogue
TV MA	Mature Audience Only. To be viewed by adults	Graphic violence	Explicit sexual activity	Crude indecent language	Intensely direct dialogue

http://www.mpaa.org/tv/content.htm

The 1980's were the I, and I alone or the Me, me, me generation of status seekers. By 1989, 60 percent of American households with televisions received cable service. Television came of age in the seventies as topics once considered taboo were broached on the airwaves for the first time. By the late eighties, TV innovations and trends included anti-family sit-coms like Roseanne and Married with Children, and tabloid TV with Geraldo, Phil, Sally, and others.

Based on the 1999-2000 PTC Network Report Card, there are no family-safe broadcast networks left. Considering the influx of adult-themed programming infiltrating the "family hour," the results come as no surprise but serve as a biting reminder of the desperate need to restore the family hour to what it once was—a safe haven for family viewing.

At the beginning of the last century, television was nonexistent. At the dawn of this new century, television is the most pervasive and powerful medium in America by any and all measures. It is almost impossible to imagine American society today without television. Television has demonstrated its indisputable power to influence perceptions, attitudes, individual behaviors, and even national and world events.

The PTC established, for the first time in a study, subcategories for six types of sexual references: oral sex; pornography; masturbation; so-called kinky practices (phone sex, group sex, and bondage); homosexuality; and genitalia.

The report compares and contrasts four weeks of prime time programming from the fall of 1989 with four weeks of programming just ten years later (1999). Among the findings:

- On a per-hour basis, sexual material was, overall, more than three times as frequent in '99 as it was in '89.
- Homosexual references, rare in '89, were mainstream in '99; they became more than twenty-four times as common during the decade.
- References to genitalia were more than seven times as frequent in '99.
- The overall number of sexual references per hour during prime time went up by over 300%.

Television can be and has proven to be harmful, addictive and destructive in the lives of individuals and family. Consider the number of hours you spend away from the things of God. Are you above or below the national average of seven hours per day? These portholes are pitfalls of entrapment. Sound the alarm and make a personal proclamation. This subtle seduction has lured many away into idleness of mind, body and spirit.

## CHAPTER FOUR

Branches of Sexual Sin

CROSS ADDICTION

You have heard the terms "cross culture," "cross roads," and "cross word puzzles." These terms highlight the presence of an intersection or are an indication that a divergence is about to take place, if it has not already happened. Remember that our definition for addiction is any compulsive habitual behavior that limits the freedom of human desire. Women with sexual sins, whether they are addicted to sex, shopping, gambling, or the Internet, just to name a few, have the propensity to be cross-addicted. There are various reasons why this dynamic takes place. The reasons often result from the increase in tolerance and the need, the drive, to get more of the stimulus to continue to feel good about the self.

- As my appetite increases, my palate has a desire to try new things.
- One addiction is not fulfilling my needs.
- I like the feeling of this other stimuli.
- I can't always meet my needs with just one addiction.
- Someone introduced me to this other addiction, now I can't shake it.

It is best to question individual clients who are sexually addicted to determine if there are other addictions in their lives with which they are also grappling. Therapists should look for extremes, compulsions, and habits, as they explore the client's thought life. We are aware that our ratio (in private practice) could be different from other practices, but our research shows that roughly 75% of sex addicts are cross-addicted. In the national survey of 600 recovering sex addicts conducted by Dr. Carnes, he highlights these statistics:

* 83% have more than one addiction themselves.

* 71% have contemplated suicide or faced severe depression.

As this research demonstrates, most sexually addicted people also face either cross-addictions or dual diagnoses. This shows that they are faced with compound problems—they are not just dealing with the sex addiction alone, and they may feel incredibly desperate and hopeless about their plight. Many of them were super-achievers or underachievers (living in extremes). They are helpless to stop their behavior, and those who make up their support system may reinforce their hopeless beliefs.

These individuals perceive themselves as flawed, bad or evil, often as a result of family messages. They are flawed, but it is from the standpoint that their beliefs are flawed—they believe that they are cracked, broken, bad or evil. They also believe that at some point they have no control over their behavior. This, of course, is irrational thinking or beguilement by the enemy, Satan.

Evil is a strong word for which we need a working definition. A little boy asked his dad one day, "Daddy what is evil?" Evil is "live" spelled backward. Evil is in opposition to life. It is that which opposes the life force. It has, in short, to do with killing. In the case of sex addicts, addiction is killing the opportunity of their freedom to choose, as opposed to simply being in bondage. This is a typical profile of how sex addicts perceive themselves.

This type of warped thinking leads to their being attracted to other addictive behaviors. They believe, "Well, I don't always act out my sexual fantasies, so I may as well do this other thing." Some addicted people feel unworthy of getting what they need in straightforward ways, so they manipulate. Even in their cross-addictions, the mindset is, "If I can not get my first stimulus (sex), then I must go to the next stimulus." "I am going to have what I intend to have and I won't stop until I get it."

Linda was struggling with a sexual addiction compounded by several cross-addictions. Linda's addiction demanded satisfaction daily but she would act out mostly from Thursday to Sunday. As her appetite grew she realized that she needed another release. She was a manager for one of the Fortune 500 companies and had a reputation of being self-driven and very productive. She knew how to motivate her employees. She created and implemented new incentives in her department, to not only keep morale high but also to keep her department leading in numbers and sales. As time went on, she realized that being a workaholic was a secondary release of her sexual addiction because she could not always have sex as much as she wanted it. So she settled for the next best thing that led her to feel good about herself.

Another way she would satisfy or reward herself was through shopping and buying nice clothing items for her self. Of course, this was justified as a necessary business expense. But Linda could wear a different suit every day for two months without dry cleaning. Each of these acts was compulsive and always led to engaging in the addiction, but soon afterwards the stimulus wore off. So Linda stayed in a cycle of acting out, hoping not to get caught or be revealed, knowing that she had a public image that did not match her private life. Let us further explain this cycle of cross-addiction.

Experts say it takes about forty days to make or break a habit. For example, Janet may be feeling a little lonely in her life. Janet will make the association in her mind that, "If I 'do' a particular behavior then I will not feel lonely." So Janet may find herself wanting to perform or act out that behavior that will relieve her loneliness. This acting out could involve others or a display of self-sex.

Those actively seeking relief from loneliness, or whatever need must be met, will develop a habit. This behavior will become entrenched into their thinking as an integral part of everyday life. They in turn become dependent on it, needing it, and wanting more of it. It may sound simplistic, but one effective way of ending an addiction is to stop the behavior, change the way the act is processed mentally and start doing something else. The key to change is to renew your mind first. Make a determination to stop. Our minds control our bodies. Secondly, replace the bad habit with a healthy habit.

You can substitute the addictive behavior for one that is productive. Remember the parable about cleaning the bad spirits (habits) out of a house (your body, God's temple)? Jesus taught that you clean the house and replace what was bad with something that is good or you will end up in a worse situation (Luke 11:26). You can read more about this in Luke, chapter eleven.

This was just simply stated, but you're probably thinking that breaking the behavior would be pretty difficult, nothing simple about that. You are correct, but it is important that we understand that we must remove the behaviors and all familiar affiliations (places, people, objects, etc.) in order to start the process of breaking the bondage.

DUAL MENTAL HEALTH DIAGNOSIS

In this section, we want you to become more aware of the various sexual disorders. Some of these disorders are being fed through media, music, and out of control moral values. We will look at two categories: Sexual Disorders or addictions and Paraphilias. Paraphilias are: recurrent, intense sexual urges, fantasies, or behaviors that involve unusual objects, activities, or situations, and cause clinically significant distress or impairment in social, occupational, or other important areas of functioning (DSM-IV). Before we continue let us again examine the difference between sex addiction and someone who has a high sex drive. ***Common characteristics of Sex Addicts are as follows:***

- They have a pattern of out-of-control behavior.
- They continue in their addictive pattern, even though it is destroying their lives.
- They will often pursue dangerous or high-risk sex.
- They are sexual even when they do not intend to be.
- They have serious life consequences because of their sexual behavior.
- Their sexual behavior affects their work, hobbies, friends, and families.
- They use sex to help them control their moods and manage stress and anxiety.

- They obsess about sexual things so much that it interferes with normal living.
- They may have periods when they extinguish all sexual behaviors and become sexually aversive. (Carnes, 1997)

If you can relate to this list, chances are there may be an addiction issue in your life, as opposed to just having a high sex drives. You be the judge. Review the list again and determine if your sexual drive is normal, high, or possibly addictive.

People with "high sex drives" may exhibit similar characteristics. However, their behavior may not cause sufficient impairment and functioning to require treatment. They may periodically connect with their partners. They are not avoiding intimacy but are more driven by their physical desire for satisfaction than their emotional need for intimacy.

Being driven excessively by sexual urges can often lead to obsession and compulsion. For example, the question was raised, "Can you be addicted to masturbation?" Yes, this is by far the most common sex addiction that is treated by clinicians. This usually is the first sexual behavior many of us will do repeatedly. This is commonly where the sexual compulsivity starts with sex addicts and often this behavior, regardless of other behaviors they acquired in their addiction, usually stays active. Pornography often follows masturbation heightening the stimulation. Pornography combined with regular masturbation is the cornerstone for most sexual addictions.

Many women struggling with sexual addiction have great difficulty recovering from this combination of behaviors. The pornography with fantasy creates an unreal world that sex addicts visit throughout their adolescence and other developmental stages. This creates a vicious cycle that controls their emotional and sexual appetite leading to dependency upon these objects and fantasies to meet their emotional and sexual desires; maybe hundreds of times before having sex with a real person. For some individuals, fantasies are standard for erotic arousal and are always included in sexual activity. The behavior, sexual urges, or fantasies cause clinically significant distress or impairment in social, occupational, or other important areas of functioning. Let's look at some of the paraphilias (sexual encounters), which you are probably already familiar with just by another name. These types indicate certain levels of sexual behavior (remember Carnes levels 1, 2, and 3).

Exhibitionists are those who want to be seen while exposing their genitals to strangers or those who least expect it. These acts can happen anywhere from a public park to an elevator. Sometimes they masturbate while exposing themselves.

Fetishism involves the use of non-living objects for sexual gratification or stimulation. Some of the common fetish objects include women's and or men's lingerie or shoes.

In **Frotteurism** the focus involves touching and rubbing against a non-consenting person. The behavior usually takes place in a crowd so that it cannot be detected.

A **Pedophile** is an individual who is attracted sexually to children 13 years or younger. The behavior is rationalized as having "educational value" for the child or by asserting that the child derives "sexual pleasure from them," or that the child was "sexually provocative."

Sexual Masochism involves the act (real, not simulated) of being humiliated, beaten, bound, or otherwise made to suffer during foreplay or during the sex act itself.

Sexual Sadism involves acts (real, not simulated) in which the individual derives sexual excitement from the psychological or physical suffering of the victim during foreplay or during the sex act itself. The sadistic fantasies involve complete control over the victim who is terrified by anticipation of the impending sadistic act.

Transvestic Fetishism involves cross-dressing. While cross-dressing, the transvestite will usually masturbate, imagining himself to be both the male and female objects of sexual fantasy.

Voyeurism occurs when a person observes individuals naked, undressing or in the process of engaging in some type of sexual activity.

With this definition, we could say that mostly all of America engages in voyeurism. With the sexual activity that takes place in the movie theaters, television, videos and the new Reality TV shows, many viewers fall into this category. There is even a new program made for MTV geared towards teens called "Undressed." This hour-long program consists of four 15-minute vignettes of various sexual situations, which end with the individuals getting undressed.

Eric Griffen-Shelly in his book, <u>Sex and Love: Addiction, Treatment and Recovery</u>, estimates that cross addictions fall into the following categories:

- Chemicals 50%
- Food 33%
- Work 25%
- Gambling 5%

Since there is a high incidence of depression found among those with sexual addictions, when diagnosing sexual addiction, it is important to rule out other mental health and personality disorders. Those with sexual addiction problems clearly demonstrate out of control behavior, but so do other diagnoses. Review the list of behaviors below and see if you can identify other possibilities based on the out of control behaviors presented:

- Exceed their intent in the amount, type, extent and duration of sexual behavior
- Pursue sexual behavior in a trance state, almost oblivious to their actions
- Pursue sexual behavior despite obvious risk and danger
- Pursue their behaviors to the point of physical injury (38%) or exhaustion (59%)
- Lead a secret or double life
- 65% run risk of venereal disease (no protection)
- 58% engaged in criminal behaviors risking arrest
- 19% were arrested

Clients who have a sexual addiction problem are often initially diagnosed with another disorder prior to the discovery of the depth of their problem. A thorough assessment during intake will assist the counselor in determining the diagnosis. Additionally, people with sexual addictions are good at masking other disorders. It may take 2-3 sessions to make a proper diagnosis. It will take several more sessions to remove all the masks. By being open, honest and forthright in their communication with a counselor, clients can help expedite this process.

Terminology is crucial. In short, counselors must be aware of the word games that those who are addicted tend to play. They will answer specifically what you ask them instead of what they know you mean—so be clear. For example "Would you like to tell me about your experiences this week?" This is not a direct enough question if you are asking about their sexual activity. The answer to your questions would probably be "No!"

If you want to know about the week, then ask, "Tell me about *your experiences this week*." Even the response to this statement may not clearly address what you are asking. The client may tell you about his health, activity on the job, disappointments with his spouse, and the sexual issues are still not addressed. As a counselor of those in recovery and those that are still in denial, I have found that I have to be prepared with crisp and concise questions and an agenda for dealing specifically with the addictive personality. Assessment tools and other resources, which will assist in this process, are found at the end of the book.

ETHNICITY AND MULTICULTURALISM

We are all born as individuals with a unique genetic design called DNA. Our genetic code is like God's fingerprint on our lives.

> *For you created my inmost being; you knit me together in my mother's womb. I praise you because I am fearfully and wonderfully made; your works are wonderful, I know that full well. My frame was not hidden from you when I was made in the secret place. When I was woven together in the depths of the earth, your eyes saw my unformed body. All the days ordained for me were written in your book before one of them came to be. (Psalm 139:13-16).*

African Americans (Blacks) as well as all nations of people are unique and distinguished by creation (God), customs, characteristics, and language. As Blacks, we are rich in customs, beliefs, traditions, food, and family.

When I was growing up in the 50's and 60's, racism was still alive and very noticeable in our communities. Our parents tried to hide the sin of racism from us so we wouldn't see its ugly face. With the Detroit riots in 1967, there was no more hiding of racism. I will never forget my mother's face as she rushed toward me as I was playing on the playground that hot weekday afternoon. The expression said one of two things: one of my brothers was hurt or in trouble or daddy was mad about something.

My mother grabbed me and said I had to come home immediately. I was confused because she was not giving an explanation for her urgency. So I asked, "Mommy, what's wrong?" She replied that a riot had started. This was the first time I heard the word "riot." My mother was not going to stop and explain this new term as we rushed home. When we arrived back at the house, I noticed all the neighbors standing on their front porches. Five minutes later I looked up and saw men with green uniforms marching down the streets with rifles; they were from the National Guard. Then I formulated in my mind what a riot was: the White man coming into our neighborhood to hurt or kill Blacks.

That was my first encounter with racism. Hate and anger were spreading throughout the city over cultural rights and the freedom to choose. This was not how the riots started, but after you dig beneath the surface you discover this was the common denominator for the hatred. I felt I was in bondage within my own house and neighborhood. Even though this is a different problem, the same results occur that are in addiction: loss of choice and enslavement by outside forces that are beyond one's control.

In the Black community we had a lot of external and internal battles. Due to our customs, characteristics, language, values, and beliefs, we just handled them a little differently from other cultures. These issues became a part of our lifestyles. The word addiction was not part of our vocabulary in the 50's and 60's. An individual who had a sexual appetite was a "stud" if a male, and "loose" if female, or simply over-sexed. It was not characterized as an addiction because that was not the terminology that was being used by the Black community. Due to a lack of knowledge and understanding of the term or of a belief that made these things "sick" or patho-logical, no one thought of getting help for just "getting off."

The language that we used to explain compulsivity was expressed in our dialect. An individual who drank too much alcohol was a "wino," "jick," or just "drunk." We didn't even refer to him as an alcoholic and definitely not as an addict. The only time we heard the term addiction was for a person using hard drugs like Heroin or free-basing Cocaine. We even had terms for those hardcore drug users: we called them a "junkie," drug addict, and "dope head "or "dope fiend."

Whatever we called them, we understood that the drug was choosing them and they had no recourse or freedom to stop their behavior without information, help, direction, and deliverance. Family support, education, and income were im-portant factors if an individual was to be able to seek help and stop acting out. Often the cycle of addiction as we know it to-day was so prevalent in the Black community that it touched almost every family. It seemed as though everyone was struggling with something, whether it was debt, relationships, drugs, alcohol or just living day to day. An easy outlet was to have a party. Feeling good, dancing, drinking, smoking marijuana, and yes having sex — all of these were a quick es-cape from reality. It was better than answering the phone and dodging another bill collector.

In the Black community, families were close knit. Male friends of the family, if older than your children, were sometimes called uncle just to include them into the family. If someone had a problem, for instance a drinking problem, we would just say, "You know Uncle Jim, he is always drinking." Another subtle problem taking place was incest. Family members were having sexual relations with other family members, adults and children.

When I think about incest it reminds me of watching Roots on television 25 years ago. The master would go down to the slave quarters and get him a woman to have sex with that night. He would violate someone because he was in a position to do so.

Unfortunately in the Black community, the extended family, which included friends, was not always like one big happy family. Uncles and cousins would violate young girls and act as if they had done nothing wrong. Take the case of Jenny who always got excited when she saw Uncle George coming through the front door. Little did she know, he was even more excited anticipating her sitting on his lap as he enjoyed the feeling of her squirming around. Jenny knew that every time Uncle George came by he would always give her money. His wallet was right there in his front pocket or at least that's what she thought. There was something hard in there. He would pull her more into his body and didn't let her get up right away.

As she got older she became aware of what was going on but she was afraid to say anything to anyone. She no longer ran to the door to greet him but would smile and take her place on his lap. He gave her more and more money. There were even nights when her mother would let Uncle George tuck Jenny in the bed. She never forgot the nights he touched her. She knew it was wrong but he would always say, "This is our secret." Little did Jenny know she was victimized by incest. She grew up becoming more and more distant with her uncle and other male members and not understanding why. Her innocence had been broken and a seed of resentment was planted.

This is the enemy's attack directly on the family to institute shame and guilt, resulting in brokenness and disconnectedness. Shame is an emotion that says, "I have done something I know I was not supposed to do and my conscious is tearing me up inside about it." Guilt is the result of shame. It is the state of one who has broken the law – you feel guilt when you break the law and you get caught. Sexual violation within families result in unhealthy relationships and bondage. A feeling of restriction, like something has you tied down, (but you don't know what) to the emotional guilt and shame that hides within our bodies and minds.

Sexual abuse within our families was going on and no one talked about it until years later when we realized that cousin Betty or Uncle Bill were constantly struggling in their relationships. In family systems, we believe the past will give us the key to unlock the doors in the present. Sex has no color barriers; the differences are how we handle the sin due to our culture and customs and beliefs. In the Black community, we gave people with sexual issues names like Don Juan's, Gigolos, Pimps, Players, Skeezers, Sack-chasers, Hussies, Ho's, Bed-hoppers or Nymphomaniacs to name a few. Due to the lack of awareness of or fear of the magnitude of these problems, many people of color covered the sin or renamed it to diminish the severity of the problem. Sexual addiction destroys relationships and families.

The enemy has a plan to destroy the family. Do we as a race handle our addictions differently from others? Yes. There is a distinction because of resources or lack of resources, customs, characteristics, beliefs, values, and education. If someone has a problem with drugs or sex, we do not talk about it, because the shame and the guilt are emotions we are not willing to recognize. We brush them under the rug and make comments like, "That is just him or that is just her." So the sins or issues of our "fathers" pass on to the second, third, and fourth generations. This is partly because we do not openly address the problems at hand.

As professional counselors, we learn about the histories of our clients. We find that many presenting problems extend far into or stem from the families of the individual. God is well aware of our sins. In the book of Exodus 34: 6b –7, it states:

> *The Lord, the Lord, the compassionate and gracious God, slow to anger, abounding in love and faithfulness, maintaining love to thousands and forgiving wickedness, rebellion and sin.*

Yet that does not leave the guilty unpunished; He punishes the children and their children for the sin of the fathers to the third and fourth generation.

King David's family is a good case study for our purposes. Let's examine his family. David had a family of six brothers and two sisters. When David was just a boy, God put his hand upon him. First Samuel 16:12b – 13 states that he was ruddy with a fine appearance and handsome features. The Lord said, *"Rise and anoint him; he is the one."* So Samuel took the horn of oil and anointed him in the presence of his brothers, and from that day on the Spirit of the Lord came upon David in power. Samuel then went to Ramah. David had skills; he killed the bear and defeated the Philistines' greatest warrior, Goliath. He spent time with God and knew the heart of God. It is said of David in Scripture that he was a man after God's own heart. The key to David's success was that he worshipped God and obeyed his commandments. There was no other king who fought and won more battles, and led by God's authority and leadership. But we are all born sinners (Romans 3:23). King David was no exception.

One spring day David was on the roof of the palace and he noticed a beautiful woman, Bathsheba. David sent someone to find out about her and to bring her to him. David slept with this woman who had just purified herself from her uncleanness and she became pregnant. Due to the fact that Bathsheba's husband was a soldier in David's army, the King sent for him so he could come home and spend time with his wife, hoping he would sleep with her. Just as David was acting here by sending for Bathsheba's husband, we always try to cover up our sins. Uriah never did sleep with his wife before going back to war. When Uriah returned to the battlefield, David had him killed. David believed he had covered his tracks but to no avail because God revealed David's sin to a prophet named Nathan. This is the account of how David's sexual appetite cost him and his family.

> *The Lord sent Nathan to David. When he came to him he said, "There were two men in a certain town, one rich and the other poor. The rich man had a very large number of sheep and cattle, but the poor man had nothing except one little ewe lamb he had bought. He raised it, and it grew up with him and his children. It shared his food, drank from his cup and even slept in his arms. It was like a daughter to him. Now a traveler came to the rich man, but the rich man re-*

frained from taking one of his own sheep or cattle to prepare a meal for the traveler who had come to him. Instead, he took the ewe lamb that belonged to the poor man and prepared it for the one who had come to him." David burned with anger against the man and said to Nathan, "As surely as the Lord lives, the man who did this deserves to die! He must pay for that lamb four times over, because he did such a thing and had no pity." Then Nathan said to David, "You are the man!" This is what the Lord, the God of Israel says: "I anointed you king over Israel, and I delivered you from the hand of Saul. I gave your master's house to you, and your master's wives into your arms. I gave you the house of Israel and Judah. And if all this had been too little, I would have given you even more. Why did you despise the word of the Lord by doing what is evil in His eyes? You struck down Uriah the Hittite with the sword and took his wife to be your own. You killed him with the sword of the Ammonites. Now therefore, the sword will never depart from your house, because you despised me and took the wife of Uriah the Hittite to be your own. This is what the Lord says: "Out of your own household I am going to bring calamity upon you. Before your very eyes I will take your wives and give them to one who is close to you and he will lie with your wives in broad daylight. You did it in secret, but I will do this thing in broad daylight before all Israel." Then David said to Nathan, "I have sinned against the Lord." Nathan replied, "The Lord has taken away your sin. You are not going to die. But because by doing this you have made the enemies of the Lord

*show utter contempt, the son born to you will die."
After Nathan had gone home, the Lord struck the
child that Uriah's wife had borne to David, and he
became ill. David pleaded with God for the child. He
fasted and went into his house and spent the nights
lying on the ground. The elders of his household
stood beside him to get him up from the ground, but
he refused, and he would not eat any food with them.
On the seventh day the child died (2 Samuel 12:1-
18a).*

David's adultery was the result of his covetousness. He
wanted and desired something that did not belong to him.
The root of lust or core of his appetite, even though he was a
great king, was insecurity. David had everything. The Lord
gave him so much; he was anointed king, had his master's
house and wives, Israel, and Judah. "If all this had been too
little, I would have given you even more." David, still in the
deepest part of his soul, lacked something that made him in-
secure. When he saw Bathsheba, that root of lust overcame
him and it took on another face, which is called power.

The power of lust is the illusion that the object of lust
can resolve the insecurity. Bathsheba was the object that
David believed he needed to satisfy his needs. The same cycle
happens in our families unless we break the cycle through
healing and deliverance or seeking help to break the cycle.

God chose to expose David's sin for all to see. *Prone to
wander, Lord I feel it. Prone to leave the God I love. Here's my
heart, O take and seal it. Seal it for Thy courts above."* I will satisfy
your needs according to my riches and glory", says the Lord.

The sin of lust was within David's bosom. Due to the
adultery and murder of Uriah these sins were passed on to
David's sons. Remember God said he would expose David's

sin before all of Israel. David's oldest son was Amnon, and he had a daughter named Tamar. As God promised, the murder and sexual sin appeared in his children. Lust was in the heart of Amnon after his sister Tamar. Beauty is a snare to many; Amnon's lust was so to Tamar. In the course of time, Amnon fell in love with Tamar, the beautiful sister of Absalom, the son of David. *"Amnon became frustrated to the point of illness on account of his sister Tamar, for she was a virgin, and it seemed impossible for him to do anything to her"*(2 Samuel 13:2). It was very frustrating to him. He was so vexed that he could not gain an opportunity to solicit Tamar that he became ill. Amnon tricked Tamar into believing that he was physically ill, while in fact he was ill with lust.

Amnon raped his sister and in the same moment hated her with intense hatred. He hated her more than he had loved her. Guilt and shame consumed him and because lust had failed he was not satisfied the moment he obtained what he believed he wanted. Tamar told her other brother Absalom what Amnon had done and Absalom burned with rage for two years. Absalom had Amnon killed to avenge the rape of his sister and to also secure for himself the position of successor to the throne.

In both incidents, King David did nothing because it just reminded him of his sins and God's mandate toward him and his family. David's account is typical within African American families as well as others. We as a people have been covering up our sins for generations. The key to our healing is to expose the sin and seek help so that we can be healed. Jesus Christ went to the cross despising its shame and taking on all our past, present, and future sins so we can receive healing. There is therefore no more condemnation for those who are in Christ Jesus, because through Christ Jesus the law of the Spirit of life set us free from the law of sin and death (Romans 8:1-2). This is the message of the gospel for all nations, Jews, Gentiles, everyone.

Sin has no respect of persons. It is the tool which your enemy, the devil, uses to kill, steal and destroy (John 10:10). Exposure is key to understanding. In counseling, we often use a tool that we call a genogram. A genogram is a representation of your family tree, both immediate and extended family, over a number of generations. We will construct a genogram of a family with a history of sexual sin and see how it was used to bring exposure, understanding, and healing to a family.

Mrs. A was asked to list particular information regarding her family in order to begin to construct a genogram. For example: dates, deaths, education, employment, ethnicity, medical experience or trauma, addictions, marriages, divorces, arrests, mental illnesses, pregnancies, physical illness, and religion. As the genogram began to reveal the family history she began to see her family in full view. As Mrs. A, along with her therapist, went over the chart to confirm accurate information, Mrs. A was invited by the therapist to take charge of her own genogram construction. It started revealing very complex and difficult information concerning the alleged sexual abuse of her children by her second ex-husband.

Therefore, the genogram process contributed to her feeling empowered as she began to better understand the origins of her guilt and shame. It was a powerful tool in helping her to realize that she needed to help her children and not be a passive participant. It also helped her shift from viewing herself as deficient to understanding her struggles within the context of her family patterns. She realized that her feelings of inefficacy and indecisiveness were understandable and ultimately contributed to the lack of control over her son's behavior.

The genogram process enabled a vulnerable parent, who questioned her own ability to protect her son, to tackle the arduous task of empowering herself to stop the family legacy of abuse (Dunn A. & Levitt M., pg. 239). This tool has helped so many that we decided to put it in the book so you can start forming a mental picture of your family.

A genogram is a tool that family therapists often use to analyze family patterns and interactions. A family genogram, which includes any history of addiction and abuse, will be very useful in helping you to identify the origin of many dysfunctional relating patterns.

We do suggest that if you suspect or know of any addictions, sexual abuses, or incest in your family to seek out a Christian therapist with understanding in this area. If you are in the metropolitan Detroit area or need a referral for your home state, feel free to contact our office, Abundant Life Counseling Center located in Farmington Hills, Michigan, at 313-201-6286.

Diagram #3A – Genogram

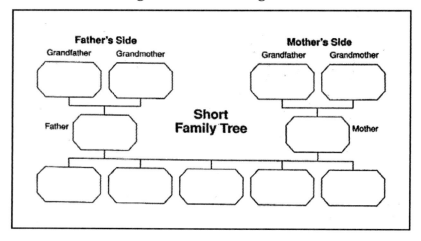

Chart #3B — Genogram Symbols

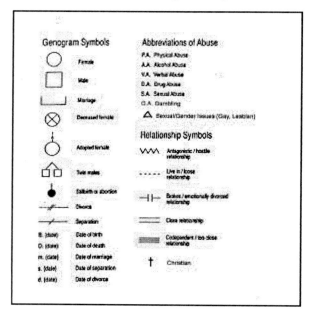

The impact of trauma in childhood often leads to sexually acting out behaviors and other addictions. Ralph Earle, in "<u>Lonely All The Time</u>" (1989) states, "When attempting to identify the sources of thoughts, attitudes, and feelings that strengthen addiction's hold on them, the sex addicts with whom we worked most commonly cited:

- One or more traumatic events during childhood— usually involving death, divorce, abuse, or victimization.
- Parents who were uncommunicative or frequently absent from the home.
- Families in which affection, encouragement, and trust were virtually nonexistent while criticism, harsh punishment, and rigid-though unwritten—rules were ever-present.
- Prohibitive messages about sex, primarily from parents.

Parents send confusing messages when they refer to sexual activity with a child which traumatizes them as playing games or when they know inappropriate games are being played and they don't intervene. Such was the case with David and his children. Amnon, Tamar, and Absalom were each devastated and never really recovered.

CHAPTER FIVE
Sista's Don't Tell

Black women are typically characterized as spiritual, strong, and secure. They tend to handle and deal with things in creative, effective ways. Black women also are viewed as confrontational, caring, and compassionate. This is not the woman you would picture as a sex addict. Surely she could find other ways of coping with the pains and hardships of life. Maybe she is just over-sexed (not an addict). Maybe she just needs the warmth of a good man.

Many women, like the woman at the well (John 4), have far too many men and the one she is with now is not her husband. Black women tend to be relational, reality based, and focused on keeping life real. They are the backbone of the family, the building block of the community, and the basic mother wit of wisdom in the church. Where does she turn for help? To whom does she cry out in her time of need, when she is struggling sexually as a believer?

LaVern's Story

Why don't Sista's tell? The reasons are many and vary among women. I heard someone say, acts that are done in the dark should remain in the dark. I was one who wanted them to stay hidden. A large percentage of women have junk in their trunk. We naturally accumulate things over the years. I arrived at a certain point where it was detrimental for me to clean my trunk. I had to move physical, mental, and emotional junk. Out of the three areas, the physical (body) was the obvious one that seemed the most manageable.

Since we can learn or unlearn behavior, habitual repetition can be put off or put on through discipline. While addiction is a stronghold that puts us in bondage, so many times I believed that if I could stop the behavior, then I would have victory. This type of counsel in and of itself doesn't give the addicted person freedom. If I stop acting out the behavior, then my mental activity or/and fantasy will continue the journey that my body was trying to stop.

Remember, the pleasure sensors located in the brain will continue to tell me or trigger my body to resume the feel good stimulation. Truly, the battleground is in the mind. I was in a major conflict. Mentally I wanted to stop but I became entangled in a ball of emotions. My emotions had more impact on me than the fact that I was a believer engaging in sexual sin. Emotions start taking over. You are thinking why are emotions so important in the addictive cycle; "I'm glad you asked."

Shame is one the strongest negative emotions that we have as human beings. It is a painful feeling of having lost the respect of others because of improper behavior. On the other hand, respect is an emotion we value. We seek to consider or treat others with deference or dutiful regard. As a woman who struggled with sexual sin, I ebbed and flowed between these two emotions as I exposed the entrapment that entangled me. Shame bares your soul and opens it before a God who loves you. Like Eve, I just wanted to cover up. I justified my behavior with pornography, masturbation, and just a few partners. Whether it was voyeurism, self-sex, one or many partners, at this point there was no justification, I was caught up in an addictive cycle.

I never considered myself to have eyes that were prone to wander. But as a teenager I was exposed to sexual nudity. I enjoyed watching people have sex. Television viewing, movies, and cable were the portholes through which I appeased my appetite for what became a steady diet of pornography. I felt justified watching others. I was set up by the pretense that watching was not always bad or harmful.

When my self-righteous attitude subsided, I realized that I was a voyeur and I could not turn off the television or myself. I took those mental pictures of others having sex around with me everywhere. One day I looked up and found myself on the Internet searching for pornographic websites. My appetite had increased to not only a habit but also an addiction; I could not shut off the TV, the Internet, or the images in my mind.

My coming out did not happen overnight. I worked on changing my behavior. Canceling cable television was easy because I could justify it by saying that I was saving money. No one had to know that I couldn't control my choice of programs to view. The Internet was harder to put off. Addressing the behavior in and by itself did not work, because my mind and emotions told my body to stay in the addiction. I realized I needed to change my mind, the way I was thinking. I no longer had the mind of Christ, but that of a slave giving in to my body. The book of Romans challenged, confronted and started me to think differently.

Therefore, I urge you, brothers, in view of God's

mercy, to offer your bodies as living sacrifices, holy and pleasing to God—this is your spiritual act of worship. Do not conform any longer to the pattern of this world but be transformed by the renewing of your mind. Then you will be able to test and approve what God's will is—his good, pleasing and perfect will (Romans 12:1-2).

My irrational thoughts became rational, gradually. I started stimulating my mind and eyes with other things. I replaced the TV with playing games in the arcade to stimulate my mind. I also incorporated board games, card games, billiards, bowling, and golf. I put off the sexual images and started stimulating my mind with new challenges. It was a struggle. I didn't need to see the live images to carry them in my mind but the signal was not as strong. Slowly my mind gained strength over my body. Reading Scripture and keeping a journal regarding the journey helped me see the addiction in a different light. The computer was a continual battle but through prayer, determination, and making right choices over and over – choosing freedom as opposed to bondage, I came out.

In the interim, however, my eyes were not the only parts of my body that wandered. As a single woman, I (LaVern) must have strong boundaries and guard my heart, soul, and senses. Yes, deliverance and healing has taken place. These struggles were in my past but I live in the present and sin is ever present around me. I'm thankful that this body has been sanctified and rededicated to our Lord and Savior, Jesus Christ.

Remember the largest playground for me as I struggled with sexual sin and addiction was in my mind. As women we have great imaginations. Soap operas and love novels are great getaways. We hide at times in other people; whether they are family, friends; or fantasies. Calling a girlfriend who has a sexual struggle was a way for me to indulge via conversation, in what is called mental voyeurism. Is this sin?

> *Although they know God's righteous decree that those who do such things deserve death, they not only continue to do these very things but also approve of those who practice them (Romans 1:32).*

Our girlfriends, family members, and sisters in Christ have or presently are struggling with sexual sin. This is the state of the flock, the body of Christ. Your sister in Christ sitting in front, beside or behind you in the pew, could be living a double life, addicted or a life of sexual struggles. I needed to find other safe women. If we confess our faults one to another, then we can start a healing process. Instead, because of shame and guilt we walk away from our healing. Jesus went to the cross, despising the shame so that we can have victory. The initial process of victory starts in our confession. Tell somebody.

As you read about our past you will choose to respect us for sharing our stories or to think about us in a shameful context. We thank Jesus that He went to the cross, despising the shame. Because of HIM we can tell the story and live righteous in Him. Sabrina and I knew that there would be a cost to writing this book. But the return has a far greater value, YOU.

Reflections

I (Sabrina) remember hearing others share their stories of abuse, adultery, infidelity, promiscuity, and other sexual sins that indicated that they were prone to wander. I thought they were so brave. How could they be so bold? I always have considered myself a risk taker, but there was so much at stake involved in sharing those deep, dark secrets. What about my image, my reputation, the ministry God had given me? I don't want to sound as if I am vain, because I know that surely we must crucify the flesh so that the new woman may live abundantly and God be glorified. But I also don't want to be a stumbling block for others. What will people think, how will they respond when they discover that I, too, have a tainted past?

I wanted to testify after each person spoke; I wanted to get it out in the open. I have a story to tell in each of those areas: abuse, adultery, infidelity, promiscuity, and other sexual sins. I have been prone to wander. The struggle to get beyond my public image kept me in bondage for a long time. Thank God there are words of hope and deliverance for those with a past:

> *That he no longer should live the rest of his time in the flesh to the lusts of men, but to the will of God. For the time past of our life may suffice us to have wrought the will of the Gentiles, when we walked in lasciviousness, lusts, excess of wine, reveling, banqueting, and abominable idolatries. Wherein they think it strange that ye run not with them to the same excess of riot, speaking evil of you. Who shall give account to him that is ready to judge the quick and the dead. For this cause was the gospel preached also to them that are dead, that they might be judged according to men in the flesh, but live according to God in the spirit".* (I Peter 4:2-6) *I take to heart the verses of scripture where Paul admonishes the believer to not be a harsh judge, but remember,* "*And such were some of you: but ye are washed, but ye are sanctified, but ye are justified in the name of the Lord Jesus, and by the Spirit of our God"* (I Corinthians

6:11 KJV).

Such *were some of you.*

Such was LaVern A. Harlin, Such was I, Sabrina D. Black. I'm sure the others that have gone before us have faced similar concerns and hesitations. Yet they told their stories. Victoria Johnson in her book, "<u>Restoring Broken Vessels,</u>" Juanita Bynum author of "<u>No More Sheets,</u>" and "<u>No Place to Cry,</u>" the Dorrie Vann Stone story. Now, Sabrina and LaVern share their stories. The aforementioned books did not specifically address sexual addiction, but told the story of how these people were impacted by sexual sin. The intent behind each of these books is to expose Satan and his attempts to destroy the people of God. They were intended to glorify Jesus Christ, the One who came to set us free from the snare and bondage of the enemy; and to help people realize that they, too, can overcome.

We really had to think through what we wanted to write about and the biblical connection to sexual addiction. We didn't want this to be just another book about sexual sin, struggles and addiction. And we certainly did not want people to read this and fall into sin.

When determining what and how much to tell, we also wanted to avoid the scarlet letter syndrome. As a people, we are quick to label and limit others. Yet, *"Therefore if any man be in Christ, he is a new creature: old things are passed away; behold, all things are become new"* (2 *Corinthian 5:17 KJV*). When people are labeled, they are made to feel as though they should wear sackcloth and ashes as an outward indication of their remorse. This extra outer show isn't necessary though because the weight of sin carries it's own mark on the sinner.

We know that the many masks worn by those with sexual addiction problems only serve to cover the pain temporarily.

We choose to remove the mask and allow others to see not where we have been but from where God has brought us. We want the world to know that no matter how deep the despair, or how devastating the downward spiral, God reaches down into the depths and delivers. It's okay to take off the mask. The healing process is accelerated when wounds are exposed to the light. Some of the many masks we have hid behind included our gifts, abilities, talents, careers, and religion. Ministry and marriage are both good hiding places as well.

Sabrina's Story

Like Stella, in a "Streetcar Named Desire," I have known for a long time that, "I always was prone to the kindness of strangers." I relied upon their generosity; their willingness to do whatever Sabrina wanted. I learned early that cute could be a curse. But I didn't know how to reverse the curse. A pretty face and a sexy body could make the strongest man weak; the wisest man, foolish; the richest man, broke; and the most faithful, lose sight of his vows. Every man I encountered was in danger of going against his own mind, heart, and soul. Sabrina was a total package. I had good looks, a come hither smile and a winning personality. I was coy, yet convincing.

When I compared myself to other girls at the time, I seemed like a saint. But in reality, I had joined leagues with the bad girls of the Bible: Jezebel and Delilah, the Adulterous woman, and others, who used their feminine wiles to prey on the kindness of strangers, friends, and foes.

As a child, I remember hearing people say, "Oh, isn't she cute, give her a lollipop (let me give her a hug, a dollar, a toy, etc)." It didn't matter what they gave me; I was getting rewarded for my looks. People would even say things like, "Can I touch her hair? It's so pretty." Just imagine the subliminal messages I received at such an impressionable age. Wow, what a concept. People will pay just to touch me.

My mother would often attempt to reverse the curse and help me realize that looks were not everything. Even before she became a Christian, my mother always emphasized character with her down home southern sayings. "Pretty is as pretty does," she would often remind me. My father models integrity and hospitality. He is an honorable man with a good name. But the world didn't seem to care as much about my name or what was on the inside as they did the pretty packaging on the outside. I never questioned my parent's love for me. I knew that I was accepted. They instilled the right moral values. But even as a child my appetite was insatiable. I wanted more. I wanted the world to love me as well.

I encounter teens now who are just like I was then: longing for more and looking to see what they can get if they just let someone look, touch, or taste what should be forbidden fruit. It may appear okay in their mind because people seem to gain something. But I will be the first to stand up and say; you lose more than you gain. The reality is you are not your own to give away. Your body and my body were both bought with a price, the life of the Lord Jesus Christ. We should not yield our bodies to wickedness – to sexual sin.

If only someone had told us and explained the truths found in I John 2:15-17. *"Do not love the world or anything in the world. If anyone loves the world, the love of the Father is not in him. For everything in the world – the cravings of sinful man, the lust of his eyes and the boasting of what he has done – come not from the Father but from the world. The world and its desires will all pass away, but the man who does the will of God lives forever."* Instead at a young age I sought to feed an appetite that will never really be satisfied by what this world has to offer.

By the time I reached young adulthood, I had become convinced that I had winning looks — prize winning looks. So, I entered one pageant after the next. As a little girl, I often envisioned myself as Miss America. What we watch on television, however, does not compare with all the things that go on behind the scene. We see the finale, after the contestants have gone through all of the pre-qualifying events. It's not all glamour and glitz.

As I look back, I want to cover myself in sackcloth and ashes. The smell of cigarettes and cigars, musty men and cheap perfume, the strong smell of liquor and bad breathe; it was all very nauseating. However, I took a deep breath and pranced through the bars week after week in high heeled shoes and string bikinis; hoping to secure enough votes to make it to the semifinals representing that bar in the next pageant. Imagine that, about fifteen to twenty practically naked young girls parading in front of drunken men. I shudder now at the thought. But back then it was no big deal. As the saying goes, "If you got it, flaunt it." And I definitely had it and knew that most men wanted it. The power associated with that type of appeal was intoxicating. It provided a very stimulating rush.

As a redeemed, Bible toting, scripture quoting, application teaching, and preaching woman of God, I'm embarrassed to think that I, Sabrina, was ever in that den of iniquity. But I was there, going through the motions with all the other contestants. God has surely brought me from a long, long, way.

This den of iniquity was not what I imagined pageant life to be. Success, however, is a powerful attraction. After winning the very first beauty contest I entered without even trying hard, I was hooked. I'm sure you have heard it said before, when asked, "Why would anyone who isn't vain enter a beauty pageant?" The answer of course is scholarship money and prizes. Okay, so I was vain too. But when selected the college campus queen over 12 other contestants, I told myself that it wasn't about looks. Preliminary screening consisted of academic excellence (3.0 GPA. or better), demonstration of talent, and the now infamous platform question. Poise and dignity were important and I knew that looks counted, but I had not focused on physical appearance in such a long time that it was not a factor for me. Being good looking was just a fact of life.

Strike a pose. One of the prizes was a complete photo session and portfolio. The flashing lights, pretty clothes, and fantasies of going exotic places as a professional model were new intoxicants. Looks were once again important. *"Vanity of vanities, saith the Preacher, vanity of vanities; all is vanity"* (Ecclesiastes 1:2 KJV). The portfolio opened many doors for local runway modeling jobs, but it never took me as far as I had hoped to go. I did meet some interesting people along the way; many of them helped me determine to get out of the modeling business before it was too late or before I went too far.

Dakota was very popular on the pageant and modeling circuits. The photographers, judges, and other contestants knew her from various events. Dakota and I first met at one of my photo sessions. We talked briefly in the lobby. Our paths crossed again at the next local pageant competition. I overheard her bragging to some of the other contestants about how her portfolio was nicer than most and it didn't cost her anything. I was intrigued.

The portfolio I won was estimated at a thousand dollars, how did she get hers free? My heart sank, as I listened to her share with the others that she only had to have sex with the photographer three times. She seemed so casual about putting a price on her body – giving herself in exchange for something (anything). I wondered how many other young ladies had slept with photographers in exchange for a few pictures. I felt dirty as I remembered myself posing before him scantily dressed in provocative positions. Thank God that there are no nude pictures of me anywhere in the world. But many of the pictures were so sensual they could have easily been Playboy centerfolds.

As I stood with the other girls huddled behind stage, waiting for the swimsuit competition to begin, I felt like I was a slave about to walk out onto an auction block. Would I go to the highest bidder, that being the judge who would cast the most votes for me? This sobering experience began my journey towards change.

Many girls unconsciously sell themselves daily. A little look, feel or even sex in exchange for a Friday night date, dinner and a movie, a trip, a new outfit. Maybe if she has sex with whomever, he will pay her pager or cell phone bill, pay her rent or car note, get her nails or hair done for her. Somehow, the word prostitution comes to mind. "Ouch."

Compliments about my looks grew old fast. Certainly I was more than just another pretty face. Pretty is as pretty does. "Maybe I should focus on what I do," I thought to myself. Doing the right thing would be easy enough. I didn't really consider myself a bad girl to start – but I was obviously comparing my behavior to the wrong set of standards.

I soon discovered that this new form of people pleasing provided it's own set of rewards. Something else to take to the limit, I developed a keen sense of appropriateness. Do everything expected and more. I became a driven workaholic, successful in every endeavor. I worked hard every day.

After all my toil and labor, I realized that it was all, meaningless. I needed more. The Corporate America package (prestige, money, and travel) provided a familiar rush. It didn't take long, however, for the tolerance to set in. I needed a new thrill. Certainly being a newlywed, owning a new home, and purchasing a new car would provide that needed stimulation and feed the need. It was great! But I wanted more.

The other executives worked hard as well, but they partied harder. Although I thoroughly enjoyed my job, all work and no play made Sabrina a dull girl. I was bored. With all the work we had to do, the other executives managed to catch happy hour every evening. They even went to house parties on the weekend. I wasn't much of a drinker any more, but I rationalized that the additional stimulus might help me relax and be more productive. Happy hour was reminiscent of the beauty pageant days. As I watched the young girls half dressed in slinky outfits: low cut tops and high split skirts, I had flashbacks.

Sitting there in my tailored business suit, it was hard to imagine that I ever dressed like that and worse, in less than what they were wearing. Now, outwardly prim and proper, I was proud of my new image. It was not until much later that I happened across the verse in Proverbs that clearly stated, *"Beauty is fading and charm is deceptive; but a woman, who fears the Lord, she is to be praised" (Proverbs 31:30).*

> *Bless the LORD, O my soul, and forget not all his benefits: Who forgiveth all thine iniquities; who heal- eth all thy diseases; Who redeemeth thy life from de- struction; who crowneth thee with lovingkindness and tender mercies; (Psalms 103:2-4 KJV).*

I began my second journey toward wholeness in 1991 at a

seminar focused on restoration. Don Crossland, a fallen leader who had found redemption, was the keynote speaker. Mark Laser, author of "<u>Faithful & True</u>" was just beginning to share his story.

God blessed, and I was privileged to present a workshop on "Unhealthy Emotional Dependency." But I was uncomfortable having my name on the brochure. What did I really know about that subject? I knew far too much. Not only was I prone to the kindness of strangers, but I was also given to extremes.

Whatever I did, or whoever I related to, I fell all the way in, to the point of worship and idolatry. I was prone to wander, and oh, how I needed the Lord to take my heart and seal it. I prepared what seemed at the time a simple outline: the concept, common concerns, circumstances leading to vulnerability, a basic checklist to identify the level of dependency, components of bondage, choosing to change, seeking counsel, and your value in Christ. Because I had personal experience with this form of bondage that often leads to further sexual sin, I came to this seminar with fear and trembling—would I be found out?

I thought again about the apostle Paul and related to his experience with the Corinthian church, and this got me through my presentation and on the road to healing that only faith in God through Jesus Christ can deliver. When I spoke at the conference, Paul's words became my reality:

I did not come with eloquence or superior wisdom as I proclaimed to them the testimony about God. For I resolved to know nothing while I was with them except Jesus Christ and him crucified. My message and my preaching were not with wise and persuasive words, but with a demonstration of the spirit's power (I Corinthians 2:1-5).

It was indeed because of God that I was able to share

any of my stories at that conference. My public ministry had just begun the year prior. This was not the time to expose any previous sins in my life, especially not those that were of a sexual nature. In the audience were members from my church. What would they think of me? How would my witness, my ministry, my fellowship be affected by what I shared that day?

THE COST OF BREAKING THE SILENCE

In 1973, Nancy Friday wrote "My Secret Garden: Women's Sexual Fantasies". Now more than twenty five years later that garden is in full bloom with Nancy's 1998—revised version of the book and "She Has a Secret: Understanding Female Sexual Addiction" by Doug Weiss. When Nancy Friday first released her book, it caused quite a stir.

She actually quoted the sexual fantasies of dozens of women, ranging from the "very common" rape fantasy to lesbian affairs to unusually explicit scenarios. It was one of the most passed around books in high school study halls (it boasted chapters titled "Insatiability" and "The Thrill of the Forbidden").

The book was taboo – the erotic detail with which she wrote was almost pornographic. Many viewed it as the only classic study of female sexuality during its time.

Over the years, the sexual fantasies of women have moved from meeting their sexual needs with an intense fantasy life of intimate relationships to sordid sex with multiple partners. In Doug Weiss' book, "She Has a Secret . . ." he clearly establishes that the range of fantasies expressed by many women is at an addictive level. Whereas Nancy sought to free women from sexual oppression, Doug and others are seeking to free women from sexual addiction. The pendulum has swung too far.

No one really wants to admit how far he or she has swung with the pendulum. Living in extremes is associated not only with addiction but instability as well. Sista's don't tell because the cost of breaking the silence is just too great. People don't relate or try to understand the dilemma you are facing; they are just judgmental. How could you? Why would you? How dare you? The moment you admit to the slightest indiscretion, you are bombarded with questions you have yet to answer yourself.

Hiding behind a mask until I was ready to answer questions seemed like a good way of responding. Masking takes on various personas that individuals undertake as defense mechanisms. When individuals come out of the closet, many have times when their experience of pressure and anxiety intensifies due to the loss of sleep, shame, loss of families, etc. This is all part of the cost that they are not sure they are ready to pay.

There are mixed reviews on whether partners should tell, how much to tell, and when. Some people believe that unless some good and useful purpose is to be served, then past occurrences should not be discussed. My mother used to always tell me, "What's done in the dark will eventually come to the light." And if that were not enough, she would remind me, "You can be sure that your sins will find you out."

These old adages served as red flags, which would indicate sin on the horizon. So even though many would say that if you got away with it, don't worry about it. I still remember her sayings. These phrases were a clarion of the scriptures that said, *"Be not deceived; God is not mocked: for whatsoever a man soweth, that shall he also reap"* (Galatians 6:7).

Because you have not suffered any adverse public consequences of your sin does not mean that you have gotten away with anything. El Roi, the God who sees, is very much aware of your sin. The accuser of the brethren will also use the possibility of your sin being exposed against you. When you have the opportunity to confess, as opposed to being "found out," you can also ensure that things are told from your perspective, not from a spectator's point of view.

If there has been unfaithfulness, one partner probably feels betrayed. Prior to any type of public confession (even if just to the spouse), the person should pray first and seek God's timing and direction. Keeping secrets can be very destructive, but sharing them can also be devastating. Private failure sometimes leads to public shame. Frank Pittman, in "Private Lies," states "dishonesty may be a greater violation of the rules (of marriage) than the affair or misconduct, and acknowledges that more marriages end as a result of maintaining the secret than do in the wake of telling."

There are times that you do tell and your marriage seems to be strengthened, only to unexpectedly die and dissipate in divorce court.

Kendra counted the cost. She asked herself the critical question, "What is the worst case scenario?" By revealing her sin, it could cost her marriage. Was she willing to suffer with the weight of guilt or the lies? Her decision cost her (more than she was prepared to pay). But in return she won her freedom from sexual sin and unhealthy emotional relationships. The breaking was in the confession and the healing was and still is as she walks with Christ.

As I (Sabrina) found myself one Sunday afternoon in church at the altar with other believers and non-believers, I heard the pastor say, "Now, go and sin no more." I knew then that God was delivering me from my own guilt and shame. The solution is not to cover up but to come out of isolation and speak up. There will be casualties along the way because we are in a war. Kendra lost the battle – her marriage, but she won her freedom over sexual sin. Satan will try to ensnare you but the key is to go tell somebody. Sista's should tell in order to be released from the bondage and hell that a secret life creates.

"Sex, Lies and Forgiveness," by Jennifer Schnieder, identifies many of the adverse consequences of disclosing inappropriate sexual behavior. She indicates that disclosure is a traumatic experience for both partners. Knowing you have been lied to is bound to cause pain; knowing you have lied repeatedly to the person you love causes guilt and shame. Adding insult to injury in most cases is the fear of having a transmitted or contracted a potentially life-threatening or incurable disease. The anger or resentment the partner feels because of this threat is sometimes insurmountable.

Among the adverse consequences spouses can expect as a result of the disclosure of the addicted person's sexual activities are:

- a worsening of the couple's relationship
- possible loss of children
- depression and even suicidal thoughts
- attempts to compensate for the pain with acting-out behaviors such as drug use and sex
- loss of self-esteem
- decreased ability to concentrate or to function at work
- feelings of shame and guilt
- distrust of everyone
- anger and rage, domestic violence
- fear of abandonment
- physical illness

- lack of sexual desires

There is much at risk. However there must be some good or value in taking such a risk. Scripture admonishes us to confess, to be truthful. When we allow God to administer grace, justice, and mercy as He sees appropriate, we experience freedom. Positive aspects of disclosure include:

- Honesty – no longer having to remember what lie you told to whom
- End of denial – ability to experience full range of emotions
- Hope for the future of relationships – learning to be in the moment with others
- Development of intimacy – a chance to get to know yourself and others better
- New start for the addict – whether in the same relationship or not
- Deeper dependence on God – walking in faith trusting God to meet your needs

> *Behold, thou desirest truth in the inward parts: and in the hidden part thou shalt make me to know wisdom. Purge me with hyssop, and I shall be clean: wash me, and I shall be whiter than snow. Make me to hear joy and gladness; that the bones, which thou hast broken, may rejoice. Hide thy face from my sins, and blot out all mine iniquities. Create in me a clean heart, O God; and renew a right spirit within me. Cast me not away from thy presence; and take not thy Holy Spirit from me. Restore unto me the joy of thy salvation; and uphold me with thy free spirit. Then will I teach transgressors thy ways; and sinners shall be converted unto thee. Deliver me from bloodguilti-*

ness, O God, thou God of my salvation: and my tongue shall sing aloud of thy righteousness. O Lord, open thou my lips; and my mouth shall show forth thy praise. For thou desirest not sacrifice; else would I give it: thou delightest not in burnt offering. The sacrifices of God are a broken spirit: a broken and a contrite heart, O God, thou wilt not despise (Psalms 51:6-17 KJV).

God has been so faithful in my life. He brought me out of a totally entangled lifestyle. He desires to demonstrate that same power of deliverance in your life as well. Trust Him to cleanse you and make you whole. Therefore confess your faults (sins) to each other and pray for each other so that you may be healed.

## CHAPTER SIX

From the White House to God's House

SEX FROM THE PULPIT TO THE PEW

Someone asked the question, "How common is pastoral indiscretion?" More than we care to talk about and the same indiscretions are taking place in the pews. If you were inside of a church standing in the balcony, as you looked down into the pews of the congregation, you may wonder, "How many people here are involved in sexual sin?" A number might come to your mind and slowly your focus turns to the center of the church where you see a single podium raised, in the center of the stage. Your focus shifts to a single voice, one man, speaking forth the oracles of God. Your heart starts to pound as his very words pierce through you.

Things that are hidden only to you start coming to your mind and suddenly you feel shame and guilt. His words are powerful as they stream through the air, exposing the darker side of the intentions of your heart. Then you realize it's not the pastor who is uncovering your sins but the Holy Spirit is convicting you. Not only is He convicting you, but everyone, from the pastor in the pulpit to the members in the pews.

"In 1988 the research department of Christianity Today,

Inc., mailed nearly one thousand surveys to pastors and 30 percent responded. According to the results of this survey, sexual temptation among pastors is a problem. Seventy percent of the respondents expressed the belief that pastors are particularly vulnerable. In the words of one respondent: "This is, by far, the greatest problem I deal with."

The survey probed the frequency of behavior that pastors feel are inappropriate. Since you've been in local church ministry, have you <u>ever done anything</u> with someone (not your spouse) that you feel was sexually inappropriate? The responses: 23 percent yes; 77 percent no. These responses would have been totally different and certainly much higher if the question were asked, "Have you <u>ever thought about doing anything</u> with someone (not your spouse) that you feel was sexually inappropriate.

The "inappropriate" behavior was left undefined. In the book of Matthew, Jesus defines inappropriate very clearly. *"You have heard that it was said, do not commit adultery, but I tell you that anyone who looks at a woman lustfully has already committed adultery with her in his heart" (Matthew 5:27-28).* That word lust continues to come up as the core of sexual sin.

To lend some perspective to these figures, Christianity Today researchers also surveyed almost one thousand subscribers of Christianity Today magazine who are not pastors (the people in the pew). Incidences of immorality were nearly double: 45% indicated having done something they considered sexually inappropriate, 23% said they had had extramarital intercourse, and 28% said they had engaged in other forms of extramarital sexual contact.

Those pastors who admitted to having had intercourse or other forms of sexual contact were asked to identify who their partners were. Their responses are listed below:

- *A counselee — someone who was seeking help (17 percent);*
- *A ministerial staff member (5 percent);*
- *Other church staff member (8 percent);*
- *A church member in a teaching/leadership role (9 percent);*
- *Someone else in the congregation (30 percent);*
- *Someone outside the congregation (31 percent).*

These pastors were also asked about the major factors that led them to this relationship. The most frequent answer: "Physical and emotional attraction" (78 percent). "Marital dissatisfaction" was a distant second (41 percent). Among professional counselors and those who work with pastors, these figures were cause for both concern and relief.

The research is clear that the masses are not aware of the large number of pastors leaving the ministry each year. Astonishing numbers have been affixed to this exodus. Various surveys show that anywhere from 20,000 – 50,000 ministers step aside from formal ministry annually. Many leave through some form of forced termination. In this study, ministers were not just pastors but other Christian leaders also (Pastors Advocacy Network, 2001).

Several years ago an article was written entitled "The War Within: an Anatomy of Lust," author's, name withheld. Let me just share a little from the article to set a certain tone.

> *I am writing this article anonymously because I am embarrassed. Embarrassed for my wife and children, yes, but embarrassed most for myself. I had a battle with lust, knowing I am not alone. Lust, like physical sex, points in only one direction. Always you want more. Paradoxically, I seemed most vulnerable to temptation when speaking or otherwise performing some spiritual service. Not everyone feels this way but a lot do. If you have not fought such obsession*

*yourself, every Sunday when you step to the pulpit
you speak to many who have, although you could
hardly read it in their blank, freshly scrubbed faces.*

Lust is the enemy that brings down so many pastors and leaders. There is a long list in our history, names you and I would recognize. Jimmy Swaggert, David Hocking, Newt Gingrich, Jessie Jackson, former President Bill Clinton, King David, and many more. There are so many, that only God knows their sins. The pulpit is such a positional platform. It sits in the middle of the church, most times, sometimes, high and lifted up. We must be careful and realize the pastor is a man who struggles just like we do.

Sexual sin is increasing monthly, weekly, daily in the churches at an alarming rate. In 1988 the percentage of sexual indiscretions were elevated more than we realized. Currently the promiscuity continues to grow.

Consider the following statistics from a 1996 survey conducted by Christianity Today International/Leadership Journal. The poll of Christian men by Promise Keepers put the figure of men within a congregation that struggle with sexual sin around 65%. Dr. Archibald Hart states in "The Sexual Man" that in his research,

- 91% of men who were raised in a Christian home reported being exposed to pornography while growing up.
- 59% of Christian men regularly fantasize about sexual relations with women other than their wives.
- 61% of married Christian men masturbate regularly (at least once per week).
- 15% masturbate to pornography.
- 33% of married, morally upright men find themselves extremely or strongly attracted to women other than their wives.

- 22%-38% report engaging in a sexual experience at work.

Do we continue to be silent from the pulpit and the pews. Bill Hybels preached a sermon series titled, "Telling the Truth to Each Other," and one illustration told of a husband talking openly with his wife about the sexual frustration that he was feeling in his relationship. That illustration telegraphed the message that it's legal in marriage to talk about sex in that way. Frustrations don't need to be pushed underground. If they are, they will eventually emerge again, just in the wrong place. Yes, telling the truth can get messy and complicated, but we need at least to try (Leadership, 1995).

We continue to isolate ourselves and cover our sin when true restoration is to confess your faults one to another so that we might be healed (James 5:16). Bill Hybels stated, "Not to preach about sex would be to desert my post at one of the most active battle fronts in our culture" (Leadership 1995). Our exhortation to pastors is to please preach from the pulpit on sexual sin before others fall. If you have been delivered and set free tell your story so others may have hope, help, and healing. *"Preach the Word; be prepared in season and out of season; correct, rebuke and encourage with great patience and careful instruction" (2 Timothy 4:2).*

We allow the lies of the enemy to keep us in bondage. Pastors believe the constant lies of the evil one. One of the biggest lies leaders believe is, "If I share my story, God will never use me again." No God will use you, but it is the good moral Christians that may try to hang you. We are an unforgiving people—mostly because of our guilt and our sin (we have just not been caught!)

Another lie, leaders believe is, "If I share my story, my fellow brothers and sisters will have no more faith in me." So these leaders live in constant fear that their sexual sins will come back on them with consequences that will shatter their worlds. So they put on the appropriate masks for the situation and slip back into the agenda we call cover-up.

If he/she knows what's good for him/her, maybe an alternative is professional Christian and or pastoral counseling. You will need a skilled counselor who can help you untangle the web of deception, set you free from your bondage, and release you at the foot of the cross—it's the only place any of us will find total peace and forgiveness!

> *For every well-known Christian television personality or author whose impropriety is widely publicized, there are any number of lesser-known pastors, Bible teachers, and para-church workers who quietly resign or are fired for sexual immorality. Most of us can name several. The myth that ministers are morally invulnerable dies slowly, however, even in the face of overwhelming evidence. But there never has been a mystical antibody that makes us immune to sexual sin. Even those of us who haven't fallen know how fierce is the struggle with temptation"* (Leadership, 1988).

Forced termination has become the term best suited for the event that removes the majority of the pastors from their work. Rarely does it separate them from their calling, but they often feel unworthy of that vocation. The months preceding the day of dismissal are filled with chaos on multiple levels. Usually, they include violent verbal abuse, traumatized emotions, threats of varied sorts, and harmful spiritual attacks. Deep exhaustion caused by dealing with the daily events, additional hours of prayer, and seeking guidance, take its toll on both the pastor and his/her entire family.

When the sad day of departure finally arrives, the pastor is without work, vision, and income. Most do not receive any form of separation pay. Too often they are simply forgotten and are alone in their pain. It is at these first crucial days and weeks that the most help should be offered, but none is given. People do not know what to do for terminated pastors (Pastors Advocacy Network, 2000).

CHANGING THE CHURCHES RESPONSE

When you hear of a pastor who has been forced from his/her ministry, do not allow them to remain alone for long. We need to find net menders and those with the heart to heal ministers and get them in contact with the injured leader. As quickly as possible inform our ministry and we will phone them and lead them through the steps to recovery, hope and renewal (Pastors Advocacy Network, 2000).

More and more churches are adopting policies regarding sexual behavior in leadership, both clergy and lay. Yet, at the same time, rare is the church that is willing to carry out church discipline, especially regarding a pastor, which is in accordance with the teaching of Scripture in Matthew 18:15-20 and 1 Timothy 5:19-22 (Armstrong, John 1995).

"Moreover if thy brother shall trespass against thee, go and tell him his fault between thee and him alone: if he shall hear thee, thou hast gained thy brother. But if he will not hear thee, then take with thee one or two more, that in the mouth of two or three witnesses every word may be established. But if he neglects to hear the church, let him be unto thee as a heathen

man and a publican. Verily I say unto you, whatso-
ever ye shall bind on earth shall be bound in heaven:
and whatsoever ye shall loose on earth shall be loosed
in heaven. Again I say unto you, that if two of you
shall agree on earth as touching any thing that they
shall ask, it shall be done for them of my Father,
which is in heaven. For where two or three are gath-
ered together in my name, there am I in the midst of
them" (Matthew 18:15-20 KJV).

"Against an elder receive not an accusation, but be-
fore two or three witnesses. Them that sin rebuke be-
fore all; that others also may fear. I charge thee before
God, and the Lord Jesus Christ, and the elect angels,
that thou observe these things without preferring one
before another, doing nothing by partiality. Lay
hands suddenly on no man, neither be a partaker of
other men's sins: keep thyself pure" (1 Timothy
5:19-22 KJV).

Following these guidelines as outlined in scripture has been a struggle and a problem throughout Christianity. At times there seems to be a double standard between the pulpit and the pew. God's Word does not contradict itself. We are the ones who compromise the situations and circumstances. This in turn sends out mixed messages to God's children, and the leadership.

Do we have to wait until our leaders are lost before we take action? Does sexual sin need to get to level three, four and five before people finally become concerned? As the people of God, we should be appalled at levels one and two. When we see our brothers and sisters on this path of destruction, bells ought to ring, red flags ought to wave, and alarms should go off. Our love for our leaders should create a sense of urgency in us that we would do whatever is necessary to help set them free.

But we wait until many are very far-gone and then we say, "I'll pray for you, I'll pray." Which often equates to I can't wait to tell someone, to slander you. And that's not to minimize the power of prayer, but we need to do something with our prayers. If we are praying in faith that God will deliver them and set them free, then we need to be willing to step in and be instrumental in that process. We can't just be praying from a distance, we need to get more actively involved. But we usually wait until the point of public humiliation, until there are broken families and ruined careers, and then we want to do something. Usually all we do then is get on the phone and gossip, talk about, read it in the papers, watch it on the TV, and we say, "Can you believe what those people did?" When we really need to be taking an active stance in helping to do something.

There are three common approaches to restoration. Assuming that the pastor or leader in question has expressed his or her need for help, restoration will be considered. Here are three common approaches to handle the problem of the fallen pastor:

1. *Immediate restoration* to pastoral office. "Immediate" is defined as fewer than twelve months after the sexual failure.

2. *Future restoration* to pastoral office after a period of time for counsel, as well as family and personal recovery. The procedure varies from church to church, but generally one to three years elapses before the fallen pastor is restored to pastoral ministry.

3. *Personal restoration* of the fallen pastor but with no possibility for restoration to office. (Armstrong, John 1995)

As evangelical Christians, we need to instill and implement policy according to God's Word. It is time the body of Christ makes a concerted effort to reach out to injured and hurting ministers who have given their best for our Savior. Too many ministers, who are forced to leave a ministry, simply disappear, are forgotten and live in loneliness. After sacrificing so much to touch people for Christ, these men and women of God deserve our best efforts in searching them out, restoring their dignity, and showing God's love for their lives.

To bring healing and renewal to one shepherd will cause an entire congregation to gather under their wings of care.

The spiritual shepherding gifts automatically gather flocks around them. They may be formal church settings with thousands, or informal gatherings of tens, it makes no difference to the Lord. Pastors are honorable gifts placed in our lives for the benefit of the Kingdom of God. We need each and every one of them to find their place of value and let the Spirit shine through them. Helping shepherds get back on the road to recovery is one of the best and fastest means to bring revival in the world (Pastors Advocacy Network, 2000).

THEREFORE NO CONDEMNATION

Jesus' response to those caught in sin was to admonish them to go and sin no more. His approach was so different from ours. There was no inquisition, no lecture, no badgery, no clauses, or conditions. An encounter with Christ was life changing. After being in his presence the person went away empowered and equipped to confront whatever was in the past of their recovery. The person was simply instructed to change and not look back. Read the following text from John 8:1- 12 (KJV):

> *Jesus went unto the Mount of Olives. And early in the morning he came again into the temple, and all the people came unto him; and he sat down, and taught them. And the scribes and Pharisees brought unto him a woman taken in adultery; and when they had set her in the midst, they say unto him, Master, this woman was taken in adultery, in the very act. Now Moses in the law commanded us, that such should be stoned: but what sayest thou? This they said, tempting Him that they might have to accuse him. But Jesus stooped down, and with his finger wrote on the ground, as though he heard them not. So when they continued asking him, he lifted up himself, and said unto them, He that is without sin among you, let him first cast a stone at her. And again he stooped down, and wrote on the ground. And they which heard it, being convicted by their own con-science, went out one by one, beginning at the eldest, even unto the last: and Jesus was left alone, and the woman standing in the midst. When Jesus had lifted up himself, and saw none but the woman, he said unto her, Woman, where are those thine accusers?*

Hath no man condemned thee? She said, No man, Lord. And Jesus said unto her, neither do I condemn thee: go, and sin no more.

Be encouraged. Those who have fallen prey to sexual sin can go and sin no more.

CHAPTER SEVEN
Breaking the Bondage

BIBLICAL STRATEGIES FOR COPING

(...happy is the woman who hears these words and does them).

Eventually the sexual addiction—the feeding of a need that will never be satisfied—becomes the governing force in the life of the person. It has been our experience—and many of our clients—that the sexual addiction can't be satisfied. Professionally speaking, addictions by their very nature are compulsive, obsessive and preoccupy the mind. Judith's addiction enslaved her and ultimately destroyed her life, and her moral will and desire. She knew the right thing to do but had no desire or discipline to do it.

Most people understand that powerful people wrestle with powerful temptations and often lose the struggle. We say its because of the illusion/realization of their "power" that has deceived them into believing that they are above the law—retribution, marital, civil, God's—you name it. You remember the stories of Samson, David, Solomon, don't you? These men—anointed men—fell into the trap of thinking that their desires were more important than anything else in their lives. You remember, too, how acting—yielding—moving to satisfy their desires led to their destruction.

their desires led to their destruction.

Admittedly, the same cycle of behavior nearly destroyed our lives. Fortunately, God through His Son, has helped us to interrupt our willful destruction and has brought us back into a right relationship with Him, ourselves, our desires, and our significant others.

As biblical counselors, we have had to remind ourselves that although the "addiction may oppress our desire, erode our will, confound our motivation, contaminate our judgment, it's bondage, it's never, ever absolute." (Gerald May, 1987). The bondage is never absolute.

If you will allow me (Sabrina) a slight digression—when I was caught up in self-absorption, I was always aware that God was somewhere near me and that I was more, much more than my desires or behavior. So, I knew it was a matter of time before my rescue. Some of you know this feeling. You sense that there is more to you, but have yet to explore what that is. You long for something that you know is far more satisfying, but it's not clear.

Well, my sister, that's God letting you know that your help, your salvation is close. Keep those feelings as near your consciousness as you can and expect God to enter your situation in a way that saves you to the utmost.

Now, the world—the materialistic system that is, in our opinion, is only partly responsible for your addiction! Satan entices you; you follow to a place of totally moral abandonment and then he tells you that you're stuck. You believe that there is no hope for you. You've heard the cliché, "once an addict, always an addict." This is a lie.

A personal friend of mine Judith (not her real name) was drug addicted. She was, past tense, because in her understanding that God in her life was far more powerful than any drug or any worldly system that suggested to her that she would always be a "recovering addict." "Naw" she would say, "God made me, saved me and I don't, I won't, spend the rest of my life being afraid of myself—relapses. I am God's child, I am free because of God's Son, and I will live in that freedom." This has worked for her. What's your take on your addiction? Will you begin now disowning it or continuing to protect it as if it is a fragile infant. Judith says she's free. Will you be free also?

Scripture agrees with Judith, it says, *"Let God be true and every man a liar." (Romans 3:4)* It also tells us in John 8:31b-32, *"If you hold to my teaching, you are really my disciples. Then you will know the truth and the truth will set you free."* And *"Him who the Son sets free is free indeed" (John 8:36).* So bondage is never absolute for those of us who are in Christ Jesus. According to the text in Isaiah 61:1, Jesus came to set the captives free.

One of the things that was difficult for me (Sabrina) was trying to reconcile in my mind that if I got away with it before, I'll get away with it again. As a Christian counselor, I now understand that during the course of treatment and recovery, individuals needed to be guided into an understanding that "God is not mocked." In other words, "Your sins will find you out." Put another way, what goes around comes around. The Lord was gracious and merciful and He gave me time to confess my sin and change my behavior. And I had to also realize that God was/is an omniscient God—He knows everything. No matter how much I sneaked, how many lies I told, or whom I thought I was fooling—God *knew and knows.*

We reference Psalms 139 to make the point that there is nowhere that we can flee from God's presence. Even when we make our beds in the depths of hell, He is there. He knows exactly what we are doing. He knows exactly where we are; He knows every thought in our minds, every word on our tongue before we speak.

Our point, God knows everything. He knows how human frailty and satanic deception has taught you that the early abuse and neglect in your life is to blame for your current addiction. He knows how you fought those vain ideations, the ideas that were leading nowhere. But gave in because giving in was just natural, it was easy. He knows stuff about you that you don't know.

But the beauty of God's knowing is that He cares about you. God is not interested in setting you up so God can punish you, He is a God of love, forgiveness and second, third, fourth, fifth... chances. Longsuffering, God is. So this issue is not what God will do to you if you don't change, but how long can you stand, withstand, a life of defeat? Sin, scripture says, when it is finished leads to death. Your choice, my sister—life or death. We chose life. And we are writing this book to say to you with the prayer, the hope, that you will join us in a new life of victory in Jesus.

This double edge sword of scripture also comforts as well. Not only does God know where we are now, but He also knows where we have been, and His love for us has been faithful. WE can also be encouraged by the fact that God knows where we are going. It's comforting to know that every day of our lives was written before any one of them came to be without free will. If it's a book that's already written, there is a beginning and an end. And, at the end, we are victorious. Although we are going through some of the difficult chapters of life right now, WE need to keep turning the pages because we haven't reached the end yet.

So how do we help break the bondage and strongholds

and begin this new life? We must first go where the problem exists, the mind. While sexual addiction generally manifests itself physically, it starts with the mind—changing the way we think. Changing the way we think requires healing the mind. Physical pleasure does not compensate for emotional hurt and spiritual emptiness.

The process of changing our mind means, for us, looking at early recollections of childhood memories, considering family systems, and analyzing belief systems. When you change your thought process, you begin to identify the things you need to focus on and avoid your focus on destructive behaviors. We are not saying avoid the thinking about the destructive behavior, which may lead to more destruction, but avoid focusing on these things.

As counselors, we believe in self-confrontation and one of the scriptures that is foundational in self-confrontation and counseling is Ephesians chapter 4:22-28. It is the basic *put off* and *put on* scripture. It also addresses renewing the mind. The scripture speaks of a thief that must stop stealing. The text asks the question, "When is a thief no longer a thief?" Now the obvious answer is, when he stops stealing. That is not enough. However, for those of you who have studied the text in depth, you know that it's not when he stops stealing, because at that point he's still a thief. He just hasn't stolen anything lately. It's when he stops stealing, changes his mind about the process, gets a job, and starts to give or do something else.

For those of us caught in an addictive cycle, "it ain't necessarily so," recovery is a process. Think about it. Take me (LaVern) for example and my pornographic indulgence. Each time I would act out in my addiction, I would vow that I wouldn't do it anymore and, of course, I did. I can't tell you how many next times I had. Then one day I kept my promise to myself. Yes, to myself, because promising God did not work! Lord knows I took full advantage of God's grace. Talk about abounding grace—I got my share. But, guess what, it worked. I got out. With the loving kindness of a God who knew me and cared for me, I got out. Through this process, my mind, desires, and behavior changed.

Sex addicts are no longer sex addicts when they stop acting out. At that point, they are still sex addicts—they are just waiting for the next acting out opportunity. I (LaVern) was no longer a sex addict when I stopped acting out, renewed my mind, and changed my mind about what I thought about sex. I became something else and started to do something else—something different, something positive and constructive. As a sex addict, just as any other addict, I had to rethink my coping strategies, learn to delay gratification of urges-develop intimacy and relational skills, and learn to communicate and resolve conflict. I needed to reprocess my feelings of guilt and shame and learn to set appropriate boundaries. I had to re-examine how I dealt with cues that provoked me to destructive sexual behavior. First, I had to become conscious of the things, the happenings that lead to my sexual misconduct. Once I became aware of the cues or signs that stirred up my desires, which often led to sexual acts, then I could get a plan of action for doing something different. For example, one of my practices was to hang out all night on Friday with friends who participated in my addiction. Well, what I decided to do, though not right away, was to spend Friday nights with my mother. After a while, Friday night had a new personality. It was different because I was *doing something different.*

Delay of gratification is the ability to wait for what you

want. While the inability to put off satisfying our desires applies to other personality types, it is critical in the life of the addict. You know this urge: you see something you want, you like what you see, there's no reason to deny yourself, so you go for it! Yeah, that's the one. Well, given your proneness, your condition, your addiction, your infantile I-want it-now attitude, your impulsiveness will cost you years of emptiness. We learned this the hard way (but is there any other way for the addict?).

Gretchen, a human resources manager at a large corporation, also learned this lesson. She stopped thinking so much about herself and started thinking about others. She began to connect with others and experience intimacy. Listen as she shares her story:

Now that my mind—my thinking—was changing, and my impulse control is operating, I am finding that I want to know people and I want to be known. I went from this self-indulgent, self-gratifying, taker to a person who valued her own worth and the worth of others—I began to care and feel. I realize through all of my selfishness that it's okay to feel and that I did not have to be afraid of being known. I did not have to run from impending hurt. Let me tell you how I got here:

One Friday I was in the middle of an all-nighter and everything was going as usual. I was getting mine and was not concerned about any one else getting theirs. I learned very early that if I did not have fun at what I was doing it would be as my mom would say, "no body's fault but my own." so I am doing my thing when all of a sudden my partner wants to talk. Talk! What-the? Something strange happened. I stopped and talk. I mean really talk. I listened too.

This was very different for me. Because in these meetings, I went to take care of business and talking was not on the agenda. But this time I talked. I had re-discovered the art of being intimate and did not know it. See I believe that as children, we learn this type of intimacy with our mothers that can be applied to other significant relationships in our lives. We who are prone to addictive behaviors, learn to ignore our need for this type of closeness. But through this ongoing process of recovery, I was beginning to re-access a very basic learned behavior—intimacy.

Of course, the ability to be intimate leads to the capacity to relate to others, period. I learned to regard other's feelings, ideas, and differences. Rediscovering myself led to an increase in my ability to communicate with others and resolve conflict without unnecessary drama — productively. I learned how to navigate conversations so that I participate in more win-win situations.

You have probably discovered that with each mental or behavioral change that you make, another positive behavior emerges. We believe this happens because we are relational beings. In other words, nothing happens without or within us without affecting our neighbors. The web of overlapping relationships makes this incidental learning possible. For example, you don't have to test fire to know that it burns. You learned it once and that was enough information for you to avoid touching it forever. The growth process of recovery is similar. For example, Gretchen learned to communicate and resolve conflicts while learning intimacy—something that experts say addicts struggle with: "Most sex addicts and co-addicts in recovery need to learn, often for the first time, how to express their feelings—especially anger—appropriately. As a rule, both have adopted a lifelong strategy of suppressing feelings and keeping secrets. Neither partner may have ever dealt with intentions or past actions. They may have no experience in bringing out their thoughts and feelings about their relationship and the significant issues that confront them either individually or as a couple. Indeed, the couple may never have dealt openly with any major issue" (Earle, 1995).

Remember Gretchen's situation, she talked and listened to her accomplice. In this single event, she exhibited the ability to communicate and resolve conflict. The conflict, though, was that she did not want to talk! Yet she rose above her selfishness to engage in meaningful conversation with a person with whom she previously had no intimate involvement. This was a significant conflict resolution—what she wanted versus what someone else wanted!

Melissa's life as a person with a sexual addiction was also confusing. The very thing that she needed was the thing that she avoided. She needed to reprocess her feelings of guilt (self blame) and shame (regret/pity). However, in order to process her feelings of guilt and shame she had to learn to be intimate which involved communicating. Think about it. The power of guilt and shame in her life was the secrecy—no one knew. She pulled it off. She got away with it. The only problem was (and there always is one) she would continue in the torment and isolation, which accompanied her self-blaming. She was not really getting away with anything. El Roi, the God who sees was aware and waiting for her to come out of darkness into the light.

A dear friend emailed me while I (Sabrina) was writing this section and informed me that she had a drinking problem. She told me that she had to tell someone or she would get caught up and perhaps go too far. For her, too far was that she would lose control and touch with reality. I asked her why did she feel the need to tell me. She said, "for accountability." She didn't want to be judged or hounded; she just wanted someone else to know what was going on with her. She said that my knowing would help keep her on track. My guess, too, was that she told me because she knew I would use my love, my knowledge, and my expertise to help her whenever she yelled. I believe that she was experiencing the loneliness and isolation of addiction, and wanted to insure that she would have someone to talk to whenever she needed. She understood the danger of total secrecy. So she broke the silence early in the process. She also learned to set appropriate boundaries, setting limits on exposure to people, places, and things that led to her addiction.

If you are really open to confronting the addiction in your life, do a genogram (family tree) to look at your family system (network). This will help you trace your family roots and give you an understanding of the levels of addiction that are in your family. It will also provide insight into areas where your family members have been prone to wander and areas you may need to watch.

For example, if we do a genogram of the Bible character King David we will discover that many of his family members struggled with sexual sin and related problems. By looking at this family's issues with sex, you will see how sin and addictions ran in their family, and possibly in yours.

However, as you examine your family system, you must also understand that your family is not the only dysfunctional family. Everybody's family is dysfunctional to some degree. We have inherited the sin nature from our first earthly father,

Adam. However, there is hope because the second Adam, Christ Jesus, has through His redemptive work on the cross, made us apart of a new family.

You may need to develop some new behavioral strategies for coping. If you think that your sexual behavior is addictive, we recommend that you seek godly counsel to help you overcome. If you are dealing with sexual addictions, you may have all kinds of problems. Some of our sexually addicted clients are dual-diagnosed. This means that they have some kind of mental health problem, such as anxiety, depression, and obsessive-compulsive behavior, in conjunction with the sex addiction.

Some people have several addictions: they may have a gambling addiction, or may be workaholics. They may have alcohol problems, or drug problems, in addition to the sexual problems. So many different things may be going on. If you came to see one of us as a client, the first thing we would do is to prioritize your needs. We would determine what problem areas are most pressing before working on the sexual addiction recovery.

Please allow us to keep our therapist hats on for a minute. In order to deal effectively with your addiction problem, you need to be careful not to take the octopus approach. Think about an octopus. It has 8 tentacles; likewise, the sex addict has cross addictions or dual diagnoses—the person—you—may have issues with masturbation, incest, or pornography. Most people, when trying to kill the octopus, attempt to cut off the tentacles. Unfortunately, what happens is that they grow back. The approach that many counselors take with counseling is to continually focus their attention on one behavioral act at a time.

For example, maybe you have struggled for years with

pornography. You begin to work through this issue and have discarded your collection of over 100 magazines. Then when you stop looking at pornography, the temptation is for you and for us to feel like we've done our jobs. And yes, we have, but this is only the beginning. This is not the time to end counseling. There are other issues to address in connection with the addiction. We cannot be satisfied with a single triumph. A few months later you come back for counseling because two other tentacles have grown in its place. You are no longer looking at pornographic magazines, but now you are obsessing over people you see on the street, having cyber sex, or calling 900 numbers uncontrollably.

Diagram # 4 – Octopus

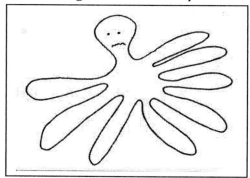

What do you need to do in order to really kill the octopus: the pornography, the fantasies, and the phone sex? We can cut off tentacles and try to address one issue at a time. A more effective, perhaps a permanent solution is to kill the octopus. Killing the octopus means finding ways to get to the root, the source of our addiction. For us, that way begins with denying the material body or natural—sinful—desires. The Bible calls it, *"crucifying the flesh."*

However, we realize that this is easy for holy-rollers to say, but it is a beginning. We also realize that preachers have been telling people for centuries to *"crucify the flesh"* and people are still living defeated, addicted lives. Below are some of the scripture references that we commonly use. The Word of God has the answers for healing our lives, and as Christian counselors we incorporate God's Word in our professional work with our clients. It is not the outer man that represents who we are. It is the Spirit of God in us Who gives us life.

> *I have been crucified with Christ and I no longer live, but Christ lives in me. The life I live in the body, I live by faith in the Son of God, who loved me, and gave himself for me (Galatians 2:20).*
>
> *If ye then be risen with Christ, seek those things which are above, where Christ sitteth on the right hand of God. Set your affection on things above, not on things on the earth. For ye are dead, and your life is hid with Christ in God. When Christ, who is our life, shall appear, then shall ye also appear with him in glory. Mortify therefore your members which are upon the earth; fornication, uncleanness, inordinate affection, evil concupiscence, and covetousness, which is idolatry: For which things' sake the wrath of God cometh on the children of disobedience (Colossians 3:1-6 KJV).*

For us, the behavioral strategies for coping that we go through are the process of "put off's" and "put on's." For example, 2 Corinthians 5:17 KJV states:

Therefore if any man be in Christ, he is a new creature: old things are passed away; behold, all things are become new." That's the focus we want our clients to have. We don't want them to spend too much time focusing on their past. Whatever happened that has contributed to or caused their present state has already happened. Yes, it is important to understand the past, but we don't want the client to dwell there. At some point, we want clients to focus on the present and determine a course of action for establishing a different future.

One of the other things that we often use with clients when helping them to do this behavioral coping is Romans chapters 6, 7, and 8. We encourages them to read these chapters' daily and take notes on what is God saying to them about their situation through the text. For those of you who have been there, done that—we offer other options later in this work. For now, hear the word of God as God has given us to minister in the lives of addicted people in our care.

> In Romans chapter 6, Paul asks the question,
> *What shall we say then, do we continue in sin that*
> *grace may abound? By no means, absolutely not."*
> *They need to be reminded that they are dead to sin,*
> *they have been crucified with Christ and the life they*
> *live in the body is no longer their life, but the life of*
> *Christ.*

When they go on to Romans chapter 7, they understand that they're not the first person to struggle with the internal conflict of good and evil waging war in their members (bodies).

> *For we know that the law is spiritual: but I am car-*
> *nal, sold under sin. For that which I do I allow not:*
> *for what I would, that do I not; but what I hate, that*
> *do I. If then I do that which I would not, I consent*
> *unto the law that it is good. Now then it is no more I*
> *that do it, but sin that dwelleth in me. For I know*
> *that in me (that is, in my flesh,) dwelleth no good*
> *thing: for to will is present with me; but how to per-*
> *form that which is good I find not. For the good that I*
> *would I do not: but the evil, which I would not, that I*
> *do. Now if I do that I would not, it is no more I that*

do it, but sin that dwelleth in me. I find then a law,
that, when I would do good, evil is present with me.
For I delight in the law of God after the inward man:
But I see another law in my members, warring
against the law of my mind, and bringing me into
captivity to the law of sin which is in my members. O
wretched man that I am! Who shall deliver me from
the body of this death? I thank God through Jesus
Christ our Lord. So then with the mind I myself serve
the law of God; but with the flesh the law of sin (Ro-
man 7:14-25 KJV).

Here, Paul gives a discourse of the good that he would do, he didn't do and the very evil that he knows not to do, those are the things that he continued to find himself doing. He finally says, *"Wretched man that I am, who will deliver me from this body of death?" And his response is, "Thanks be to God."*

We try to make it clear that it is the grace of God that has set us all free. Ours is really a life of thanks to God. Unless God is part of the recovery process, changes are temporary. You can make some temporal changes. Go to counseling, cut off a few tentacles, and you go away feeling better. But in order to make long-lasting, permanent change, you need to kill the octopus. You need to know that you can live a new life—a victorious one.

When we look at Romans chapter 8, we understand that *"there is now, therefore, no condemnation for those who are in Christ Jesus."* The enemy will continue to remind you of who you used to be and what you used to do. This is his job, to get you to go running back to your old behavior, wandering back to where you started. And then, bam, you have landed in a full-fledged relapse. Now you are living in the newness of life in Christ Jesus, under His control, walking immune to the enemy's temptations. I (LaVern) can remember a number of times when I thought I was well on my way to recovery and decided to have lunch or play golf with an old partner—bad idea. This single act led me to fantasize all over again. Then back to masturbation. Everyone is different, so you will have to figure out what you can and cannot handle in your recovery walk.

As part of the relapse prevention, you will need help to walk in the newness of life. In Galatians chapter 5:1, we are told to not allow ourselves to be entangled again with the yoke of bondage. *"Do not allow yourself"* is a phrase that is critical. It indicates that we have a choice here. It says do not let yourselves, don't walk into that, don't let yourself be entangled again with the yoke of bondage. You are now a new person.

In listening to some tapes a couple of weeks ago, we heard this analogy that we thought was perfect for people who are coming out of any type of addictive behavior. It talked about the witness protection program. When you think about the witness protection program, usually the people involved are guilty or a witness to some crime of another person. No question, as a sex addict we were guilty. But under the witness protection program, we came forward, and we confessed our sin; we confessed and we cooperated. Then we were given a new identity.

When we got the new identity, we were given a new name, a new birth date, a new location, new friends, and a whole new identity—a whole new life. This is what we mean by walking in the newness of life. When people accept the grace of God through Christ, they are born into a whole new family. This family, unlike the other one is not only functional; it allows persons the benefit of continual healing and cleansing— complete recovery.

Admittedly, the possibility of relapse is always present on the outside as well as on the inside. Remember the words of Paul. Let's look as some of the ways that evil presents itself on the outside.

So you are in the witness protection program. As you remember who you are in Christ, with your new birth and your new identity, the Lord protects you and someone from your old life approaches you and says: "Weren't you a prostitute?" Now is the time to live out the Scripture that says, *"Let the redeemed of the Lord say so."* Tell them who you are now. Remember the past is in the past and you have a new life. If you must respond you can say, "Excuse me, are you talking to me?" Oh, Debra died a few months (or years ago) my name is Michelle. No defense just let them know who you are and whose you are "nuf said." Remember, satan is your enemy and an accuser of the brethren.

Make no mistakes about it: there will be some spiritual warfare involved. You need to understand that, *"We wrestle not against flesh and blood, but against principalities, against powers, against the rulers of the darkness of this world, against spiritual wickedness in high places" (Eph 6:12 KJV).* There is a war being waged for your life because your soul is secure. And since your soul is secure, the war is on to keep you in addictive bondage.

There may need to be some healing and deliverance. A lot of people who come to see us say, "Well, you know, I have been through a healing and deliverance ministry. I don't understand why I am still having these problems." We need to help people understand how to walk in their deliverance. If you've been set free, quit looking back—remember this requires a change in thinking. The enemy will constantly remind you of whom you used to be. The other thing people need to know is that they will live in the body of flesh until the day they die. The flesh desires to do wrong. But, your spirit desires the things of God. Those two are walking in opposite directions. Your mind and your body must be yoked with each other to win the battle over addictions.

Galatians 5:16 says, *"If we walk in the Spirit, we will not fulfill the lusts of the flesh."* It did not say we would not have them, it just said we would not fulfill them. So please understand that. So, if you are feeling tempted, find another distraction. And then remind yourself that you are a new creature in Christ.

In the process of becoming who you are in Christ you have to stop being who you were in the flesh. As you reverse the curse and break the bondage of sexual addiction, each of the areas listed below needs to be exposed to the light of God's word during the course of treatment:

1. A pattern of out of control behavior
2. Severe consequences due to sexual behavior
3. Inability to stop despite adverse consequences
4. Persistent pursuit of self-destructive behavior
5. Ongoing desires or effort to limit sexual behavior
6. Sexual obsession and fantasy as a primary coping mechanism
7. Increasing amounts of sexual experience because the current level of activity is no longer sufficient.
8. Severe mood changes around sexual activity
9. Inordinate amount of time spent in obtaining sex, being sexual, or recovering from sexual experience
10. Neglect of important social, occupational, or recreational activities because of sexual behavior.

Accepting a new identity, knowing and using the Word of God, and understanding the spiritual nature of this warfare are ways you will need to move toward recovery. Another way is to "talk to us." In our experience, catharsis (the expression of pent-up feelings) is a key component in counseling those with sexual addiction. Many who are struggling have a history of relationships that have been devoid of intimacy. Consequently, they have not had much experience expressing their true emotions. Sexual misbehavior was their way of expressing whatever emotions they might feel. One client told us, "When I was angry, disappointed, sad, depressed, anxious, fearful, exhausted, overwhelmed, or frustrated—I'd watch pornography and masturbate. What better way was there to celebrate?" Or so they thought. These behaviors led to an avoidance of dealing with the pains of life or connecting with others.

However, when I finally sat in session and gave voice to the feelings behind my mask it provided great relief. When I expressed feelings, it seemed to release energy that had been tied up, and I felt freer. Although talk therapy was often healing, it was only a beginning. It was important that I do something other than talk about things; I needed to do something differently.

Recovery is the process of choosing to change; then following the new course regardless of the obstacles. To recover is to get back something that is lost or stolen; to get (oneself) back to a state of control, balance or composure; to reclaim; to catch or save oneself from a slip, stumble, self-betrayal. (Webster, 1988). These are all things that the recovering sex addict needs to do. Recovery brings with it a sense of urgency. However long the client has been in bondage to the addiction, it is far too long. We need to help clients take back what the enemy has taken from them—their freedom to choose.

SPIRITUAL WARFARE / HEALING-DELIVERANCE

As Christians first and therapists second, we always need to go into a session battle ready. Understand who the enemy is first. Clients are powerless over their addiction, and the enemy, the devil, does not want them to walk free from their addiction. It is a possibility there might be relapse many times over before healing is experienced, but remember *"the battle is not yours it's the Lord's"* (2 Chronicles 20:15b) and that means victory.

Understand in spiritual warfare, that it is a byproduct of war that there will be some casualties. We can't win all of them. But by understanding the enemy, weapons, territory, and tactics we will gain back a lot of the land. We can recover! When Jesus Christ returns for His Church, the body of Christ will experience no more pain, hurts, and addictions. Comfort your clients with this hope as they walk to the road of recovery.

The enemy (Satan) came but to kill, steal, and destroy. The enemy is waging war for your mind, body, and soul. The struggle to be set free from the bondage of sexual sin and addiction is spiritual warfare.

We cannot only seek physical solutions to a spiritual problem. That is why we integrate the Word of God and prayer into our treatment plan. The Bible is clear in telling us *"Our struggle is not against flesh and blood but against the rulers, against the authorities, against the powers of this dark world and against the spiritual forces of evil in the heavenly realms"* (Ephesians 6:12).

You cannot fight a battle without proper weapons. Remember that addiction is a state of compulsion, obsession, or pre-occupation that enslaves a person's will and desire. Addiction sidetracks and eclipses the energy of our deepest, truest desire for love and goodness. We succumb because the energy or our desire becomes attached or nailed to specific behaviors, objects, or persons (May, Gerald, 1988). We have to admit first and foremost that we are powerless over the addiction and our lives have become unmanageable. Secondly, come to believe that a power greater than ourselves could restore us to a normal way of thinking and living. Thirdly, make a decision to turn our will and our lives over to the care of this power of our own understanding.

This power is Jesus Christ and the Word of God. A sexual addict is out of control and needs healing and deliverance with Christ.

RELAPSE PREVENTION/ WALKING IN THE SPIRIT

Renewing the mind is one of the most critical phases of relapse prevention. In I Corinthians 10:13 we are reminded of a key concept in recovery.

> *No temptation has seized you except that which is*
> *common to man; and God is faithful, he will not al-*
> *low you to be tempted beyond what you are able, but*
> *with the temptation will provide a way of escape also,*
> *that you may be able to stand up under it.*

In recovery people need to know that the place of escape is the mind. In other words, when your life takes some unexpected turn, your mind begins to find ways to cope so that you can deal with the new happening. Now, when your mind was a slave to sin, your goal was to appease your impulses with some inappropriate sexual act. However, now that your mind and your will are subject to the spirit, your desires are open to the righteousness of God. Once I understood this fact,

I began to find things — Godly things—to focus on. I learned to think on the pure and lovely things—the things of good report. This small exercise made a great difference in my thought life—my constant thoughts and imaginings. For every temptation begins as a thought. Our mind is a battleground. Paul admonishes us in II Corinthians 10:5 to take every thought captive to the obedience of Christ. Using the Word can do this; literal quotes from scripture to assist us.

So what I (Sabrina) began to do was quote scripture to encourage myself. It worked supernaturally for me! It also worked for Doreen. When Doreen was in college, she used to entertain obscene phone calls. When the call came, usually early in the morning (3:00 am) she would answer and participate in the caller's perverse conversation. But once she understood that this was destructive behavior, she began quoting scripture to the caller. At first, he would listen and try to use his sexual language to drown the Word of God. But she hung in there until he hung up the phone. Once he realized that all he was going to get was the Word, he stopped calling. James 4:7 KJV says, *"Submit yourselves therefore to God. Resist the devil, and he will flee from you."* You can use the Word of God—the Spirit's Sword—to fight this battle.

Learning to resist is key to recovery. The initial temptation is usually the strongest. Press through those first few minutes. This brings to mind the words to the song, *"Yield not to Temptation . . . for yielding is sin. This victory will help you, some other to win. Fight manfully onward, dark passions subdue. He is willing to aid you. He will carry you through."*

CHAPTER EIGHT
The Process of Recovery & Rebuilding

A recovering addict likened it to a tide: "It is either coming in or going out, and it never stands still" (Griffen-Shelley, 1998). Recovery is an active process. And you must see it as a voluntary act of consciousness. You want to always be moving forward in your recovery. Allow us to reiterate the words of the apostle Paul:

> *Brethren, I count not myself to have apprehended: but this one thing I do, forgetting those things which are behind, and reaching forth unto those things which are before, I press toward the mark for the prize of the high calling of God in Christ Jesus (Philippians 3:13-14 KJV).*

Our challenge, and yes, our prayer for you is that you continue forward on your journey, never looking back.

It's a beautiful thing to know that you have hope and in that hope God is standing at the finish line with His arms open, waiting to congratulate you on a race well ran. As professional counselors and as instruments of God, we want to encourage you to seek professional help to make your journey a smoother one. It is our hope that the content of these pages has moved you to, at least, think more seriously about your recovery. Below we offer some ideas to consider as you make recovery a reality. The first is thinking about your primary goals for recovery.

There are several possible goals for treatment. The following items are not exhaustive but serve as a starting point for you. Of course, each of these items may be tailored for your specific need.

- Establish sobriety /abstinence from acting out behaviors
- Break through denial in each area of life being impacted by this life dominating-sin
- Explain the nature of the addiction, including cycle, levels, bondage, and deliverance
- Surrender to God's process in accordance with the Word for being set free
- Develop support system, accountability plan, and discipleship goals
- Confront the accuser of the brethren regarding guilt and shame
- Grieve losses and establish new life
- Improve intimacy in family and other relationships
- Establish appropriate boundaries for any and all former triggers

A second recommendation to consider in the process of recovery and rebuilding is to beware of the counselors that you choose. Admittedly, we have fellow counselors who we would not seek for counsel. Some of us become so haughty. So consider getting second and third opinions. Above all, pray and trust yourself. One of the best indicators of a good counselor is compassion. Remember the scripture: *"Brethren, if a man be overtaken in a fault, ye which are spiritual, restore such an one in the spirit of meekness; considering thyself, lest thou also be tempted" (Galatians 6:1 KJV).*

A counselor who is aware of his or her own faults is your greatest asset. One thing we both discovered in the process of this writing is that we both can be pretty harsh judges. And Paul reminds us, "And such were some of you." All of us were delivered and set free from something. What we found was that we had forgotten that we were once addicts and to some degree still struggle with one form of addiction or another. We hasten to say, our walk today is a victorious one. However, in our forgetfulness, and in our relief that we no longer walk in addiction, we realized that we were not applying the grace of God to others that had been applied to us. God has forgiven us of much, and, (of much) we are grateful. Since yours is a road that we both have traveled, please know that we feel for you. Our desire is to see you on that road less traveled.

Another way to make a sound decision in choosing a counselor is to watch for reactions as you tell your story. What kinds of questions are asked? Are they asking what I call, non-essential or nosey questions? You know questions that focus on content—what happened—and not process—what it all means in your recovery. Some counselors can be guilty of what we call mental voyeurism. Mental voyeurism occurs when counselors are aroused, or experience vicarious pleasure when clients tell their provocative sexual stories. The key thing to remember is to stick to the necessary details; just the facts.

You must also be aware of your reason for providing unnecessary details. You may find that sharing your story arouses you. This requires your active listening to yourself. Ask yourself, "Is this information necessary, or am I caught up in the story?" Establish boundaries within your mind prior to counseling. Pray for the Holy Spirit to protect your mind against these potential hazards. If you know that your counselor has a personal history of sexual addiction, you will be well within your rights to ask them where they are in their recovery, and if seeing you will compromise their ability to be effective. It is important that you both know your limitations.

Be aware of your language. Given the nature of this addiction there are bound to be some uncomfortable moments. Just speak as clearly as you can and in your own language. In other words, talk your normal talk. Having a discussion about word usage will be helpful. Engage your counselor in an honest discussion about her or his comfort level with your verbiage.

Again, you may challenge your counselor on his or her word usage. Counselors, especially Christian ones, have a tendency to use technical language as a way to keep the talk "clean" or professional. Let the counselor know if you don't understand what they mean. A good counselor will use your language, so this may not be a problem. Let's hope you don't get a prude who will gasp at the sound of slang verbiage. Let's hope he or she knows that they will not lose their salvation if you cuss.

Finally, you may want to consider using as many supporters as possible. At the end of the section is a list of books that we recommend. There are some Internet sites for sexual addiction, several organizations, and several support groups. There are many resources available in the field. But none can take the place of a properly trained professional.

When you seek help from a trained professional, remember that they are not the change agent – God is. Although the counselor is a trained and experienced professional, rely on God. Believe us, that is what we do. We don't know all the answers, but as we pray, God gives insight, revelation knowledge, and words of wisdom to help guide the course of treatment. We use various spiritual disciplines including scripture, prayer, meditation in session and in our preparation for therapy.

We tell the clients up front that our counseling is biblically based and unless the Lord shows up, we are useless. We are accountable to God for our service to you. One day God will confront us about our service. We desire to please God in our work.

Since God will confront us about our service to you, you should know that confronting the addict is a large part of what we do. So, prepare yourself for it. We are confrontational because we care and we desire to bring about change. Expect homework. All of our clients know right up front that we give homework, lots of it. Some of it is indeed busy work, but all of it is designed to benefit you. Your time with us is not the "magic hour."

The mystery of transformation, change, is what happens between sessions—what happens after you walk out of our offices. One of the most powerful things about homework is that it helps you to focus on and experience the reality of God in your life. This process will help you to deepen your dependence on God. Guiding you to draw nearer to God is at the heart of what we do. The Word of God, tools, resources, homework, and psychotherapy incorporated with prayer is the process of recovery.

Identify the things that trigger setbacks. This can be difficult because you have habits that set you on a downward spiral (of which you are not aware). For me (LaVern) it was driving down a certain street. It took me a while to realize it but the route that I took to work was filled with suggestive material (billboards) so that by the time I got to work, I did everything but work. My mind was held captive so that I spent most of the day in fantasyland. So, keep a journal. What happens before and after taking these sexual freedoms?

And remember, to leave an addictive lifestyle, there are numerous triggers and weights you need to lay aside. For example, if pornography was a problem, you may need to monitor all reading materials, especially those with pictures of partially dressed woman or men (eg. Sports Illustrated— swimsuit edition, Victoria Secrets catalogue, numerous women's magazines). You may also need to monitor your exposure to many television programs, movies and videotapes. You may decide to watch only programs that are for a general audience. Here's a key scripture to remember:

> *Let us lay aside every weight, and the sin which doth so easily beset us, and let us run with patience the race that is set before us, looking unto Jesus the author and finisher of our faith; who for the joy that was set before him endured the cross, despising the shame, and is set down at the right hand of the throne of God. For consider him that endured such contradiction of sinners against himself, lest ye be wearied and faint in your minds (Hebrew 12:1-3 KJV).*

Finally, strengthen your relationship with God. Working on this relationship is a process that continues until the day of Christ Jesus. So intensify your efforts and learn more about God and His Word. *"Wherewithal shall a young man cleanse his way? By taking heed to do according to Thy Word. With my whole heart have I sought thee: O let me not wander from thy commandments. Thy word have I hid in mine heart, that I might not sin against thee"* (*Psalms 119:9-11 KJV*). Remember the Word is a powerful tool; speak it into your life for wholeness.

FAMILY THERAPY

As an addictive person, you will need as many supporters as possible. This is why we recommend family counseling, especially for married clients. Many spouses tend to feel that it is his or her fault. Your spouse will want to know what more should he or she do? Some wonder: "Should I have sexual relations with my spouse more? Is there something wrong with me?" While these are admirable questions of concerned mates, no one is to blame. In the work of recovery, there is no place for blaming.

Your spouse can be the worst in the world, that is no excuse for your behavior. On the Day of Judgment, God will not accept our minimizations, rationalizations, or justifications. We will not be able to blame-shift as Adam tried to do in Genesis 3:9-12 KJV. When Adam had sinned and God confronted him about it, he said, *"The woman whom thou gavest to be with me, she gave me of the tree, and I did eat."* Like Adam, you may have made some poor choices and each choice has a certain consequence. However, though you may suffer some of the consequences of others choices, you are not responsible for their choices. Part of our work with your family is helping them to understand that your sexually acting out behavior is not their issue necessarily. However, it does affect them both directly and indirectly—you are in a relationship. Remember, you are connected because of it.

The Bible says, *"that two are better than one because they have a good reward for their labor"* (*Ecclesiastes 4:9 KJV*). When one falls the other can pull them up. Both of us have fallen in the process of recovery but there was always one helping the other. Family support, in addition to professional counseling, may serve to help you get up. There is a contemporary gospel song by Donnie McClurkin titled, "Get Back Up Again." The message of the Bible is to get back up and walk in the power of God's Spirit. As we have been working through our own recovery, the Lord has helped us, to help others. *We are so mindful that it is always the gratification of the flesh that compels us, but it is the grace of God that constrains us, and it is growth in God that controls us.*

Our healing was not simply for us but for you and many others reading this book, ***Prone to Wander: A Woman's Struggle with Sexual Sin and Addiction.*** We have talked to amazing women who have had similar battles living with addiction; some won, some lost. The Lord has allowed us, two African-American women to share a message of hope, help, and healing. If you are (as we were) prone to wander, we hope that this resource will help you as you move toward recovery. We are living witnesses that if you choose to walk in the power and freedom of victory through our Lord and Savior, Jesus Christ, you can get back up again. To God be the glory!

Counseling Tools & Resources

Counseling Tools

Chart #4 — The SAST – Sexual Addiction Screening Test

The Sexual Addiction Screening Test (SAST) is designed to assist in the assessment of sexually compulsive or "addictive" behavior. Developed in cooperation with hospitals, treatment programs, private therapists, and community groups, the SAST provides a profile of responses which help to discriminate between addictive and nonaddictive behavior. To complete the test, answer each question by placing a check in the appropriate yes/no column.

YES   NO

☐   ☐   1. Were you sexually abused as a child or adolescent?

☐   ☐   2. Have you subscribed or regularly purchased sexually explicit magazines like Playboy or Penthouse?

☐   ☐   3. Did your parents have trouble with sexual behavior?

☐   ☐   4. Do you often find yourself preoccupied with sexual thoughts?

☐   ☐   5. Do you feel that your sexual behavior is not normal?

☐   ☐   6. Does your spouse {or significant other(s)} ever worry or complain about your sexual behavior?

☐   ☐   7. Do you have trouble stopping your sexual behavior when you know it is inappropriate?

☐   ☐   8. Do you ever feel bad about your sexual behavior?

☐   ☐   9. Has your sexual behavior ever created problems for you or your family?

☐   ☐   10. Have you ever sought help for sexual behavior you did not like?

☐   ☐   11. Have you ever worried about people finding out about your sexual activities?

☐   ☐   12. Has anyone been hurt emotionally because of your sexual behavior?

☐   ☐   13. Are any of your sexual activities against the law?

☐   ☐   14. Have you ever made promises to yourself to quit some aspect of your sexual behavior?

☐   ☐   15. Have you ever made efforts to quit a type of sexual activity and failed?

☐   ☐   16. Do you have to hide some of your sexual behavior from others?

☐   ☐   17. Have you attempted to stop some parts of your sexual activity?

☐   ☐   18. Have you ever felt degraded by your sexual behavior?

☐   ☐   19. Has sex been a way for you to escape your problems?

☐   ☐   20. When you have sex, do you feel depressed afterwards?

☐   ☐   21. Have you ever felt the need to discontinue a certain form of sexual activity?

☐   ☐   22. Has your sexual activity interfered with your family life?

☐   ☐   23. Have you been sexual with minors?

☐   ☐   24. Do you feel controlled by your sexual desire?

☐   ☐   25. Do you ever think your sexual desire is stronger than you are?

• 1989 from *Contrary to Love*
Patrick Carnes, Ph.D.

Chart #5 — Family Adaptability

	RIGID (Very Low Adaptability)	STRUCTURED (Low to Moderate)	FLEXIBLE (Moderate to High)	CHAOTIC (Very High)
LEADERSHIP (Control)	Authoritarian leadership. Parent(s) highly controlling.	Primarily Authoritarian but some equalitarian leadership.	Equalitarian leadership with fluid changes.	Limited and/or erratic leadership. Parental control unsuccessful, rebuffed.
DISCIPLINE	Autocratic, "law & order." Strict, rigid consequences. Not lenient.	Somewhat democratic. Predictable consequences. Seldom lenient.	Usually democratic. Negotiated consequences. Somewhat lenient	Laissez-faire and ineffective. Inconsistent consequences. Very lenient.
NEGOTIATION	Limited negotiations. Decisions imposed by parents.	Structured negotiations. Decisions mainly made by parents.	Flexible negotiations. Agreed upon decisions.	Endless negotiations. Impulsive decisions.
ROLES	Limited repertoire: strictly defined roles.	Roles stable, but may be shared.	Role sharing and making. Fluid changes of roles.	Lack of role clarity, role shifts, and role reversals.
RULES	Unchanging rules. Rules strictly enforced.	Few rule changes. Rules firmly enforced.	Some rule changes. Rules flexibility enforced.	Frequent rule changes. Rules inconsistently enforced.

Chart #6 — Summary of Treatment Processes

	ASSESSMENT	INTERVENTION	TWELVE STEPS	TREATMENT	RECOVERY
BELIEF SYSTEM	Determine catalytic events and catalytic environments	Affirm person using illness concept	Challenge core beliefs and restore new ones	Provide process for restructuring belief system	Integrates new core beliefs
IMPAIRED THINKING	Elicit rationalizations and distortions of reality.	Confront gross defenses and work towards acceptance of "illness."	Confront impaired thinking.	Develop feedback mechanisms to keep reality in focus.	Recognizes ongoing need for feedback.
PREOCCU-PATION	Determine priority obsession modes.	Teach role preoccupation plays in addiction and co addiction	Support grieving of loss of pathological relationship.	Develop new coping strategies to deal with anxiety.	Has awareness of personal limits.
RITUALS	Identify specific rituals.	Place injunctions on rituals.	Supply new rituals through sponsors, meetings and readings.	Create life enhancing rituals.	Perceives new ritual as passage to new phase of life.
BEHAVIOR	Determine extent of pattern of sexual behavior.	Set contractual limits.	Provide new coping behaviors.	Assist in establishing sobriety.	No longer sees sex as the enemy.
DESPAIR	Check for life-threatening depression.	Connect client and family members with Twelve Step sponsors.	Restore healthy shame and guilt.	Establish relapse prevention strategies.	Has no secret life.
UNMANAGE ABILITY	Search for evidence of "out of control" behavior.	Use unmanageability as leverage to commit to help.	Initiate second order change to disrupt system.	Develop recovery plan to support manageability.	Manageability reflects acceptance of self and need for others.

Chart #7 — Emotional

MAD	SAD	GLAD	AFRAID	ASHAMED	LONELY
Bothered	Down	Secure	Uneasy	Uncomfortable	Out of Place
Irritated	Blue	Relaxed	Apprehensive	Awkward	Lonesome
Annoyed	Low	Contented	Cautious	Self-Conscious	Disconnected
Steamed	Lonely	Satisfied	Tense	Embarrassed	Invisible
Irked	Disap-pointed	Pleased	Anxious	Sorry	Insignificant
Frustrated	Melan-choly	Optimistic	Nervous	Apologetic	Ignored
Angry	Unhappy	Happy	Distressed	Remorseful	Neglected
Fed Up	Dissatis-fied	Encouraged	Scared	Guilty	Separated
Disgusted	Mournful	Cheerful	Frightened	Disgusted	Isolated
Indignant	Grieved	Thrilled	Alarmed	Belittled	Unwanted
Enraged	Depressed	Delighted	Overwhelmed	Humiliated	Rejected
Irate	Crushed	Joyful	Frantic	Violated	Deserted
Outraged	Empty	Elated	Horrified	Dirty	Outcast
Furious	Despair-ing	Overjoyed	Petrified	Defiled	Desolate
Pissed Off	Devas-tated	Ecstatic	Terrified	Degraded	Forsaken

The following are the most current addresses for the <u>sex addiction support groups</u>:

Sex Addicts Anonymous (SAA)

P.O. Box 70949

Houston, TX 77270

(713) 869-4902

Sexaholics Anonymous

P.O. Box 111910

Nashville, TN 37222-1910

(615) 331-6901

Sexual Compulsives
Anonymous (SCA)
Old Chelsea Station,
P.O. Box 1585
New York, NY 10013-0935
1-800-977-HEAL

Sex and Love Addicts Anonymous (SLAA)
P.O. Box 119, New Town Branch,
Boston, MA 02258
(617) 332-1845

Sexual Recovery Anonymous (SRA),
PO Box 73, Planetarium Station,
New York, NY 10024
(212) 340-4650 or:
PO Box 72044
Burnaby, BC V5H4PQ Canada (604) 290-9382

The following locations are <u>places of refuge where hurting pastors and church leaders</u> can find help.
Center for Continuing Education
Richard Busch
Episcopal Theological Seminary in Virginia
Alexandria, VA 22304
703-370-6600
Its centerpiece is a six-week renewal and growth program for ecumenical clergy. Offered three times a year, the program provides a period of reflection, learning, discovery, confirmation, and deepening of ones faith.

Eagle's Nest Retreat Ministries

John Gowins
P.O. Box 437
Ouray, CO 81427
800-533-4049

Eagle's Nest offers professional counseling and vacations at minimal cost to ministers and their families. Ouray is located in the beautiful San Juan Mountains of southern Colorado.

Focus on the Family – Pastoral Ministries Department

H. B. London, Jr.
Roger Charman
8605 Explorer Drive
Colorado Springs, CO 80920
719-531-3347

Offers resources, referrals, and face-to-face consultation. Provides an audio tape subscription series called "Pastor to Pastor," regional gatherings, tapes, booklets, and a weekly fax letter called "The Pastor's Weekly Briefing."

Pastor's Advocacy Network

Inclusion on this list does not imply endorsement. Neither the authors nor the publishers can accept responsibility for the actions of any person or group listed. If you know of additional places of refuge that offers special care for God's anointed, please write to the authors. Your resources will be included in the expanded version of this text.

References

Anderson, Neil T. (1998). <u>A Way of Escape: Freedom from Sexual Strongholds</u>. Harvest House Publishers, Inc.

Arterburn, Stephen. (1995). <u>Addicted to Love: Understanding Dependencies of the Heart, Romance, Relationships, and Sex</u>. Servant Publications.

Arterburn, Stephen, Stoeker, Fred, Yorkey, Mike. (2000). <u>Every Man's Battle: Winning the War on Sexual Temptation One victory at a Time.</u> Waterbook Press.

Blinder, Martin. (1999). <u>Fluke.</u> Permanent Press.

Bloomer, George. (1998). <u>Oppressionless.</u> Blooming House Publishers.

Carnes, Patrick J. (1992). <u>Don't Call it Love: Recovery from Sexual Addiction</u>. Bantam Doubleday Dell Publishing Group.

Carnes, Patrick. (1983). <u>Out of the Shadows: Understanding Sexual Addiction.</u> APA = p. 265 4th ed Minneapolis, MN: Compcare Publishers

Cavanaugh, Simon. (2000). Presidential Black Mistresses: Thomas Jefferson Port. Available: http://classicals.com/federalist/ThomasJeffersonhall/messages/152.html (December 16, 2000)

DeRamus, Betty. (1998). Presidential Sex Scandals Aren't New: It's the Lie that Gets to Us. Available: http://www.detnews.com/1998/accent/9808/20/08200025.htm (December 16, 2000)

Dobson, Edward G., Dollar, Truman. (1995). Restoring a Fallen Colleague. Leadership Journal, 92, 106-121.

Downs, Hugh. (1999). Sins of the Fathers: When Did We Come to So Glorify Gossip? Available: http://archive.abcnews.go.com/onair/insite/insite980917_downs.html (December 16, 2000).

Dunn, A.B., Levitt, M.M. (2000). The Geneogram: From Diagnostics to Mutual Collaboration. Family Journal: Counseling and Therapy for Couples and Families, 8, 3, 236-244.

Earle, Ralph, Osborn, Kevin, Earle, Marcus R. (1995). Sex Addiction: Case Studies and Management. Brunner/Mazel Publishers.

Earle, Ralph. (1989), Lonely All The Time. New York: Pocket Books.

Goetz, David L. (1995). Sins of the Family. Leadership Journal, Summer 1995, 52-65.

Grenz, Stanley., Bell, Roy D. (1995). Predator, Wanderer, or Lover: What Types of Pastors are Vulnerable to Adultery — and How to Avoid a Fall. Leadership Journal, Summer 1995, 35-36.

Griffin-Shelley, Eric. (1992). Sex and Love: Addiction, Treatment and Recovery. Greenwood Publishing Group, Incorporated.

Griffin-Shelley, Eric. (editor). (1993). Outpatient Treatment of Sex and Love Addicts. Greenwood Publishing Group, Incorporated.

Hybels, Bill. (1995). Preaching that Oh-So-Delicate Subject: Speaking About Sex Clearly and Redemptively is One of the Preacher's Biggest Challenges. Leadership Journal, Summer 1995, 43-48.

Johanson, Mary Ann. (1997-98). Elizabeth and Mrs. Brown. The Flick Filosopher. Available: http://www.flickfilosopher.com/flickfilos/archive/4q98/elizabethmrsbrown. Html

(December 16, 2000)

Kasl, Charlotte Davis. (1990). Women, Sex, and Addiction: A Search for Love and Power. Harper Trade.

Kirk, Jerry. (1995). A Way of Escape: Winning the Personal Battle Against Porn. Leadership Journal, Summer 1995, 85-88.

Laaser, Mark R., Smalley, Gary. (1996). Faithful and True: Sexual Integrity in a Fallen World. Zondervan Publishing House.

Levin, Jerome David. (1998). The Clinton Syndrome: The President and the Self-Destruction Nature of Sexual Addiction. Prima Communications, Inc.

Long, Tom. (1998). Chat Room: Presidential Affairs, Flings Come to Mind on this Holiday. Available: http://detnews.com/1998/accent/9802/16/02160009.htm (December 16, 2000)

Means, Marsha. (1999). Living with Your Husband's Secret Wars. Fleming H. Revell Company.

Moeller, Bob (editor). (1995). The Sex Life of America's Christians. Leadership Journal, Summer 1995, 30-31.

Murphy, John A. (2000). The Indictment. Brockston Publishing Company.

Roberts, Ted. (1999). Pure Desire: Helping People Break Free from Sexual Addictions. Gospel Light Publications.

Ruben, Douglass H. (2000). Over-Sexed and Under-Loved: A Recovery Guide to Sex Addiction. IUniverse.com, Incorporated.

Rutter, Peter. (1989). Sex in the Forbidden Zone: When Men in Power-Therapists, Doctors, Clergy, Teachers, and Others-Betray Women's Trust. Jeremy P. Tarcher, Inc.

Shaumburg, Harry W. (1992). False Intimacy: Understanding the

Struggle of Sexual Addiction. NavPress Publishing Group.

Shaw, Andrea. (1996). Seen That, Now What?: The Ultimate Guide to Finding the Video You Really Want to Watch. New York, NY: A Fireside Book:

Shepard, Alicia C. (1999). Gatekeepers Without Gates. Available: http://ajr.

Newslink.org/ajrlisamar99.html (December 16, 2000).

Stebben, G., Morris, J. (1998). Should a Catalogue of Presidents' Sexual Escapades Comfort Clinton? Available: http://cgi.cnn.com/books/news/9808/20/.

Presidential.hankypanky.cnn/ (December 16, 2000).

Stebben, G., Morris, J. (1998). White House Confidential: The Little Book of Weird Presidential History. Cumberland House Publishing.

Straussner, S.L. (editor), Zelvin, Elizabeth, (editor), (1997). Gender and Addictions: Men and Women in Treatment. Jason Aronson Publishers.

Travine, Sheldon. (1995). Compulsive Sexual Behaviors. Psychiatric Clinics of North America 18 (1) 155-169.

Unknown. (1995). Traits of a Sexually Healthy Pastor. Leadership Journal, Summer 1995, 19-26.

Wade, Linda R. (1989). Warren G. Harding: Twenty-Ninth President of the United States. *Encyclopedia of Presidents.* Children's Press.

Weiss, Douglass, Debusk, Dianne. (1993). Women Who Love Sex Addicts. Discovery Press.

Weiss, Douglass, Debusk, Dianne. (1998). She's Has a Secret: Understanding Female Sexuality. Discovery Press.

White, John. (1993). <u>Eros Redeemed: Breaking the Stronghold of Sexual Sin.</u> InterVarsity Press.

Whiteman, Thomas (Tom). (1998). <u>Victim of Love?: How You Can Break the Cycle of Bad Relationships.</u> Pinion Press.

We'd Like to Hear from You!

If you would like more information concerning the Prone to Wander Series of books, would like to have the authors conduct a workshop, or if your church and/or organization would like to sponsor a symposium at your facility, please contact us at:

Abundant Life Counseling Center
31275 Northwestern Hwy #249
Farmington Hills, Michigan 48334
313-201-6286

Email: Sabrina D. Black   jadebooks@aol.com
           LaVern A. Harlin   lavernkimbrough@sbc.net

If you would like to share your successes, problems, tips, secrets, solutions, or experiences, please write to us at the above address. Please include permission to quote you in other writings. Topics of particular interest:

- People, places and portholes that have led you astray from your walk with God
- How this text helped you in your recovery or in helping someone else with their recovery
- Other addictions, ie., gambling, Internet, food disorders, drugs, etc.
- Unhealthy emotional dependency, same sex relationships, and or abusive relationships
- Other resources (ie., books, videos, workshops, etc.) that you have found useful in your recovery

Thanks and God Bless You
Sabrina and LaVern

About the Authors

Sabrina D. Black

Sabrina is the CEO and Clinical Director of *Abundant Life Counseling Center,* an outpatient mental health facility, which emphasizes spiritual values. Among her credentials, Mrs. Black is a Limited Licensed Professional Counselor, Certified Addictions Counselor and Certified Biblical Counselor with 14 years of experience in individual, family and group counseling. She has degrees in Psychology and Counseling. Sabrina has expertise in the fields of Gambling Addiction, Sexual Addiction and Sexual Abuse and issues relating to Clergy and Ministry Leaders. Mrs. Black is adjunct faculty at Ashland Theological Seminary, and Cornerstone University. She is president of the National Biblical Counselors Association, and chairperson for the Black African-American Association of Christian Counselors. Elder Sabrina D. Black is a national and international speaker for conferences, retreats and workshops. *Sabrina's goal is to help God's people live the Abundant Life through hope, help, and healing!*

Other Books by Sabrina D. Black

HELP! for Your Leadership
Healing, Encouragement and Loving Perspective for Overwhelmed Leaders
ISBN: 0-9703634-6-X

Can Two Walk Together?
ISBN: 0-8024177-1-X

Counseling in African-American Communities
ISBN: 0-3102402-5-5

LaVern A. Harlin

LaVern is a single woman who has a heartbeat to help God's people walk out of bondage and into freedom. LaVern is a Certified Biblical Counselor and has a degree in psychology. A teacher, counselor, writer and speaker, she brings the Word of God alive through visual illustrations and practical demonstrations. A speaker at home, locally, and globally, LaVern travels as a missionary to Africa. She is also the director of Global Projects for Hope, Help and Healing, a faith based community service organization that serves to empower and assist minorities who experience economical, mental health and social problems. Her heartbeat is doing the work of the ministry and preparing God's people to walk in their calling. *"God has given us all that we need to finish the work and finish well."*

Book Order Form

Prone to Wander:
A Woman's Struggle with Sexual Sin and Addiction

Name _____

Address _____

City_____ State _____ Zip _____

Phone _____ Fax _____

Email _____

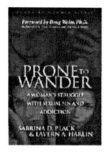

Quantity	
Price *(each)*	$14.99
Subtotal	
S & H *(each)*	$2.99
MI Tax 6%	

METHOD OF PAYMENT:

☐ Check or Money Order (*Make payable to*: **Abundant Life**)

☐ Visa ☐ Master Card ☐ American Express

Acct No. _____

Expiration Date (mmyy) _____

Signature _____

Mail this form with payment to:
Abundant Life Counseling Center
31275 Northwestern Hwy #249, Farmington Hills, Michigan 48334

For faster service:
Phone   313-345-9524
Fax   313-345-9531
Email   jadebooks@aol.com